"In a manner soundly doctrinal, deeply spiritual, and engagingly contemplative, *God Is Love* penetrates beyond the 'left'-'right' culture wars and beneath the surface of things into a fresh appreciation of the lavishness of God's love. This book is truly a gift."

— Bishop Richard J. Malone, ThD, STL
Chair, U.S. bishops' Committee on Evangelization and Catechesis

"Insightful, poetic, and challenging."

— Kevin O'Neil, CSsR
Associate Professor, Systematic and Moral Theology
Washington Theological Union

"This is a beautifully written, pastorally attuned, and gently thought-provoking book. A wide range of readers will enjoy the clear and accessible language, with minimal technical terminology, together with the lightness of touch with which Kelly treats the themes. While robustly orthodox, this creative experiment in communicating the essence of Christian faith will prove a most useful resource for adult education, faith development and introductory theology programs, inspiring its readers to freshly own, live and further explore their faith."

— Professor Anne Hunt, FACE, OAM
Executive Dean, Faculty of Theology and Philosophy
Australian Catholic University

"In *God Is Love*, Anthony Kelly, CSsR, provides a reflection on divine Mystery, clearly and simply written, that will leave you breathless. This book should be in the hands of anyone who has faith, or who wants to have more faith."

— Bill Huebsch
Director, PastoralPlanning.com
Author of *Grace: God's Greatest Gift*

God Is Love

The Heart of Christian Faith

Anthony J. Kelly, CSsR

A Michael Glazier Book

LITURGICAL PRESS
Collegeville, Minnesota

www.litpress.org

A Michael Glazier Book published by Liturgical Press

Cover design by Ann Blattner. Illustration courtesy of iStockphoto/ Thinkstock.

1	2	3	4	5	6	7	8

Library of Congress Cataloging-in-Publication Data

Kelly, Anthony, 1938–
    God is love : the heart of Christian faith / Anthony Kelly.
        p.   cm.
    "A Michael Glazier book."
    Includes bibliographical references and index.
    ISBN 978-0-8146-8043-8 — ISBN 978-0-8146-8044-5 (e-book)
    1. God (Christianity)—Love—Meditations.   2. Catholic Church—Doctrines—Meditations.   I. Title.

BT140.K455   2012
231'.044—dc23   2012004548

Contents

Focus and Dimensions

 This sequence of reflections offers an outline of a workable theology while at the same time suggesting a contemplative focus for Christian spirituality. Theology is always in progress, but it is ever beginning from, and ending in, the great mystery of God's love that is treated here. As Pope Benedict wrote in 2005 in his first encyclical letter,

> "God is love, and he who abides in love abides in God, and God abides in him" (1 John 4:16). These words from the First Letter of John express with remarkable clarity the heart of the Christian faith: the Christian image of God and the resulting image of [humankind] and its destiny. In the same verse, Saint John also offers a kind of summary of the Christian life: "We have come to know and to believe in the love God has for us."[1]

This little book is, I hope, a reasonably clear and concise exposition that is not too academic. To that purpose footnotes have been kept to a minimum, and the language, as far as possible, does not deal in technicalities. The imagination and erudition of a great army of theologians are always developing what we treat here only in basic outline, though it is unlikely that any future theological developments will be in radical contradiction to what follows in these short chapters. Still, in treating this focal point of Christian faith in this particular way, we dare to hope that the faith we share will emerge as ever new, so as to be freshly owned, lived, and further explored.

There comes a time when those of us who are usually involved in the complexities of theological research feel the need to express what matters most as simply and tellingly as possible. It has long been pointed out that it is the custom of the New Testament itself to compress the manifold meaning of revelation into a short formula. There are many examples of this, and the one we have focused on here is the Johannine statement "God is Love." We have tried to unpack this concise and profound expression by exploring seven terms that are necessarily implied in the Love that God is—the trinitarian terms, *Father, Son, and Holy Spirit*; the *cross* and *resurrection* as events within the paschal mystery; the *church* as the revelation of God's love being worked out in history; and finally, the ultimate hope for *eternal life* and heaven itself.

The purpose of this little book is to meet at least one theologian's need to say things as clearly and tellingly as possible. More importantly, especially in these days of dialogue on many fronts, there is a need to have a formulation from which to set out and to which to return. Dialogue between different Christian communities, let alone between different religious faiths, is not helped if there is unnecessary confusion in what Christian faith means or if the focus is blurred.

There is a further reason. By compressing the meaning of Christian faith into the single sentence that is the point of convergence of seven terms, we can assist theology to remain *theo*-logy, especially for those embarking on theological studies. With all the demands of current theological developments on so many fronts and with all the wonderful resources now available, it is easy to leave God out, as it were. The divine Mystery is everywhere implied, but not exactly as the limitless, living communication of love and freedom. It takes some effort to keep the focus sharp and the framework of thinking clear. Hence, we offer this small book as a kind of working theology, a theology always in progress yet with a clear starting point and aim. It is capable of being endlessly expanded even while retaining a clear, robust doctrinal outline.

I will say more about this in the first chapter. For the moment let me thank friends and colleagues who have encouraged me to write something more accessible for them and others. I thank especially my Redemptorist confreres, Dr. Marsha Skain, Mary Ann Brandt and family of Mankato, MN, and the dean of our faculty, Professor Anne Hunt. This little project was encouraged from the beginning by the staff of the Liturgical Press, Hans Christoffersen as publisher, and, toward the end, purged of inelegancies and errors by the sharp-eyed but ever-sensitive copy editor, Eric Christensen. My thanks to them and to all involved in the production process of this small book on the greatest of themes. I hope that it will shed some light and reflect a spectrum of colors as it is read in the many, quite different contexts in which the Christian people pray and think and hope in the ever-changing world.

The infinities of God's grace in Christ are never exhausted. In response to this gift, it is always time for a more creative catholicity on the part of the church in its mission to all nations. How that will work out so as to inform and inspire future generations can only be a matter of hope. On the other hand, as history goes on and as our faith meets new challenges, further dimensions of the great truth will be revealed: "God is Love."

CHAPTER 1

Love, the Focal Point

"God is love" (1 John 4:8, 16) is undeniably a basic statement on the character of God revealed in the New Testament. Admittedly, the word "love" does not figure in any of the creeds. And yet John's declaration, when all is said and done, is the most fundamental of all "articles of faith." Not only the Johannine writings but also the whole of the New Testament, along with the creeds formed in the centuries to follow, are expressions of the faith and hope that wholeheartedly celebrate the revelation of Love—the Love that God is. To emphasize the identification of God with love as John's letter has it, I will, where the context allows, refer to God's self-revealing and self-giving action as Love, with a capital L. Only by surrendering to Love and cooperating with it can we hope to understand it more fully.

I

In order to articulate how God is Love, a basic vocabulary of seven interrelated terms is necessary. Each of these is named in the Creed—and in the New Testament generally—with the words, *Father, Son, cross, resurrection, Holy Spirit, church,* and *eternal life*. As the meaning of these terms converge, the statement "God is Love"

1

is like a hologram. It can be looked at from various angles, and yet all its dimensions interweave, whatever the perspective, to give a sense of the whole.

In fact, depending on the context, the meaning of how God is Love unfolds from any one of the seven terms just mentioned and shows that all the others are implied. Though we might use equivalent terms in our own or other languages, no one of these focal aspects can be left out without mutilating the whole shape of Christian faith. When each of these seven terms is given its due and allowed to interact with the others, all of them together form the outlook of faith. They suggest a basic overview of all that is implied in the distinctive Christian vision and so offer a coherent sense of how God is Love.

When the meanings of these words are brought together and interact, they convey the "catholic" (*kat'holou* = "openness to the whole") sense of who and what God is, as Creator and Redeemer. As one way of keeping the "-holic" in "Catholic," this approach counteracts any fundamentalism or doctrinaire narrowness. It invites all believers to appreciate what is central to their faith and how it shapes the Christian horizon of living and acting.

If we are to give an account of the hope that is within us (1 Pet 3:15), our vocabulary must include at least the equivalents of these seven key terms in explaining reality of the Love that God is. By naming God as *Father*, we confess that God is Love and is the source of all loving and giving. As Father, God is the primordial Love, the source and origin of all loving and giving in the most personal and unconditional sense. Yet it is not possible to say everything all at once. The Love that is the source of all gifts and of all giving will be disclosed only in the course of reflecting on the other terms involved. For instance, we name Christ as the *Son* to indicate the extent of God's self-giving. By giving and revealing himself in the Son, the Father communicates what is most intimate to himself. For the only-begotten Son is most involved in God's identity as Father. Then the *cross* indicates the limit to which the love of the Father and the Son has gone. Love has not been changed into something else in its exposure to evil and rejection. It has kept on being Love so that in the *resurrection*, the transforming and truly divine power of Love is displayed in human history in a singular event that anticipates what is to come. To speak of the *Spirit* is to identify the Love that God is as continually self-giving, in eternity and in time. God's loving is not only a once-and-for-all event in our historical past but also a transforming energy communicating itself in all times, places, and lives. The *church*, too, expresses the divine source and character of Love, for it is that part of the world that has been awakened to the all-embracing mystery of Love at work. The mission of the church, in all its words and deeds, its Sacred Scriptures, its liturgy and sacraments, and its living witness, is to communicate what it has received on behalf of all. Finally, *eternal life* (or heaven) indicates the final consummation to which God's love is leading, in a universe transformed.

While these seven terms, or their equivalents, can be presented in different sequences, none of them can be omitted without mutilating the message of the Gospel or diminishing the range of hope it inspires. Moreover, the meaning of each term depends on all the others. If any one is frozen and set against the rest, a distorted picture emerges. The hologram flattens out, as it were. Furthermore, when the seven terms in question cease to condition one another, one will tend to predominate to the detriment of the interrelated whole. The simplest example of this would be to so concentrate on God as *Father* that the defining relationship of the Father to the Son is missed, and God is reduced to some kind of cultural "father figure." Conversely, if we concentrate on the *Son* in an exclusive way, we can overlook that his deepest identity is to be from and for the Father. On the other hand, some might be tempted to see all that is distinctive in Christianity in the *cross*. If that is the focal point, God's self-revelation can appear like defeat at the hands of evil and leave us with little hope and a rather morbid kind of faith. In reaction, we might argue that the *resurrection* is the defining moment. But that cannot be grasped without the recognition that it is the Jesus condemned, tortured, crucified, and left dead and buried who is raised up. Likewise, it can happen that some might be tempted to exult in the gift of the *Holy Spirit* and in the joy and liberation that are the Spirit's gifts. As a result, it is possible to forget that the Spirit is always leading us to Christ and the self-giving love he exemplifies. In a mood of defensiveness, some might be tempted to see the essence of their faith in the *church* and to become so immersed in ecclesiastical questions that the reality of church as a sacrament of God's trinitarian love is all but overlooked. Finally, we might be so intent on presenting the Christian message as the promise of an *afterlife* in heaven that it would be possible to overlook that life before death is already changed, in that even now we possess in anticipation "the life of the world to come." Already Christian believers receive the sacraments of the church. They have been baptized into Christ, conformed to him, nourished with his eucharistic Body and Blood, and possessed by his Spirit, and they participate in his mission.

Clearly, distortions can happen, and the hopeful and holistic proportion of the meaning of "God is Love" can suffer. The only solution then is to keep all our seven terms in play. If that is the case, a healthy sense of the inexhaustible and ever-active Love of God is progressively formed in our minds and hearts. It overflows into all aspects of Christian life. It is the horizon in which the church, as the living pilgrim community of faith, lives out its history in every age. This is to say that the ecology of the Christian life cannot be respected unless it is expressed in accord with the multidimensional reality that our seven key words convey.

What these names, words, or terms mean cannot be clarified by simply looking them up in a dictionary. The meaning of each one goes beyond any particular definition in the routine world of words. They each look to a unique reality so original and limitless that it remains impossible to express it in any adequate manner. All the more reason, then, why each of these seven terms needs to resonate with the others if language is to communicate what most needs to be communicated, if it is to convey a coherent and refreshing sense of Christian existence.

II

In the short chapters that follow, we will be continually emphasizing the basic character of the vocabulary we have selected. *Father*, *Son*, and *Holy Spirit* are personal names; *cross* and *resurrection* name events that mark the extremes of Love in Christ. The term *church* names the communion of believers made one in the unity of the Trinity itself and invites all to a personal sense of faith, belonging, and responsibility. And *eternal life* denotes the fulfillment of Christian existence in communion with God and in a transformed world. At that point, the personal reality of each and all is fully actualized in the vision of God and in the communion of saints.

This basic vocabulary is not made up of general or abstract terms. It is part of the language of faith that employs the most personal names by which the divine Three are invoked. It resonates with reference to the Word Incarnate and derives from the Scripture and liturgy of the church—itself an identifiable reality in history. It is the vocabulary of hope that looks to its fulfillment in the life of the world to come.

Admittedly, there is a limitation in focusing on Christian life in this particular way. What the life of faith consists in cannot be reduced to a kind of image—even a holographic image. The problem is that in outlining a neat, schematic image, the living reality of the believer is left out and relegated to the role of a spectator contemplating what might be an attractive image or pattern from the outside. That might have its own limited value, but it cannot replace a sense of being a participant in the "Love-life" that is being revealed:

> Beloved, let us love one another, because love is from God; everyone who loves is born of God and knows God. Whoever does not love does not know God, for God is love. (1 John 4:7-8)

In fact, each of our seven terms and all of them taken together can mean something only for those who, in faith, hope, and love, enter into the universe of God's life-giving love, nourished by its realities and breathing its atmosphere.

Even that can sound all too remote from the struggling, suffering, and morally ambiguous world in which the church must live and that each of us experiences. It is, therefore, important to insist that each of the seven terms of the vocabulary of Love is a summons—a call to conversion, a summons to a change of heart and to the risk of taking the Gospel seriously. Each term interrupts our usual perception of what such words routinely signify in the everyday world of communication. Each of these terms is a call to "lift up your hearts" to the unimaginable Love that draws life into a limitless horizon.

III

The seven terms plot a movement from darkness to light. In a world in which science has given us some inkling of the immensity of the physical universe, people today can feel adrift in a world of enormous proportions, as though floating meaninglessly in incalculable dimensions of space and time. When science speaks of the evolutionary dynamics of the emerging universe, our seemingly solid world appears fantastically random in its every component. Our minds are bemused by so much that is contingent and accidental in our planetary existence. The question is urgent: Where—on earth and in the intricacy and immensity of the cosmos—is meaning to be found?

Moreover, the enormity of evils the world suffers or causes can be soul destroying. The news media confronts us daily with innumerable catastrophes and communicates cosmic anxieties. What, then, of evil? That terrible question lurks in any positive or hopeful affirmation of life and love. Disease, catastrophe, the perversions of human freedom, and death itself permeate what God has created. If belief in God's love is the first and last word on creation, how is it, why is it, that evil is such a force, such a presence? Why is the wonderful mystery of creation burdened with such a problem?

The history of Christian thinking largely leads to silence and waiting. We human beings would have more chance of hearing silence and seeing darkness than of understanding evil. It is the oppressive absence of the good we need and seek. The creeds of faith attempt no philosophical answer. In the end, Christian faith offers no solution except to open the way to a more complete surrender to the mystery of Love, in order to participate in its healing and transforming. The workings of "almighty" Love remain beyond human comprehension. But when exposed to our problem of evil, the excess that Love has shown is displayed in the incarnation, suffering, and death of the Son. Love has already triumphed over evil in the resurrection of the crucified. And Love shows patience. It makes time for the whole of human history, promising a day of a final, universal judgment when evil will be revealed for what it is and brought to nothing. In the meantime, the omnipotence of Love assures us of the forgiveness of sins and promises an ultimate transformation in the life in the age to come.

There is, then, no instant solution for the conflicts and clashes, the destruction and limitations, the disease and ambiguity we experience. But the creative and healing Love that God is promises an ultimate judgment. It looks to a universal moment of truth when God's ways of creating and guiding our world to its fulfillment will be revealed.

As faith waits for this final evidence, it is summoned to stand with Jesus. He is the divine Son, who "for us and our salvation" has immersed himself in the cosmic process. Thereby he made himself vulnerable to the risk and tragedy of human history. A suffering creation finds its hope in the knowledge that God, in the delicacy and sympathy of Love, suffers our sufferings even more than we do ourselves.

IV

The Canticle of Daniel (Dan 3:57-88, 56; NAB) calls us back from cosmic sadness to the defiant affirmation of cosmic praise. The inspired writer summons all the works of the Lord to bless the Lord. In our present knowledge of the wonder of the universe and the emergence of life within it, such praise can be extended into a thousand other forms. The biblical prayer of praise runs through the realities of the natural world—sun and moon and stars, night and day, heat and cold, sea and dry land, wind and rain, animals and birds and fish, angels and human beings. Today, the contemplative appreciation of the universe leaps to new possibilities. God can be glorified in the uncanny providence that guided the universe through its amazingly improbable journey to the present. At this moment, it brings us forth to an awareness of the vast, intricate scope of the universal event.

"Bless the Lord, all you works of the Lord" (Dan 3:57; NAB)—cosmic forces, galaxies in their billions, matter in all its varied forms, consciousness in all its glimmerings, both the sturdy predictabilities and the strange spontaneities of nature, its order and its chaos, all the ten million species of living things with whom we share this planet, every instant of the billions of years that have gone into our making, all the elements of the stardust from which we are made. And as each religious community reciting the Divine Office responds after each verse, "to him be highest glory and praise forever."

At some level of our awareness we are forced to ask, Where does hope lie? The possibilities of global communication have been marvelously extended. But what, in the end, do we wish to communicate? How do we belong together? When the face of the church is disfigured by many scandals and conflicts, what is the inexhaustible source of continuing renewal? In the present time of interreligious dialogue, what is the all-embracing, gracious horizon in which the peoples of all faiths can meet with mutual respect and shared hope? In a time when the poor are with us in still-increasing numbers, in whose name and for what reason must we reach out to them in compassion?

The meaning of God as Love is not found in some fantastic bubble of religious sentiment floating far above and away from the evils we suffer and cause. Rather, it is crystallized in resources that are given us to face life in all its darkness and problems. Here, too, we have a sober reminder from John's letter:

> Whoever does not love abides in death. . . . We know love by this, that he laid down his life for us—and we ought to lay down our lives for one another. How does God's love abide in anyone who has the world's goods and sees a brother or sister in need and yet refuses help?
>
> Little children, let us love, not in word or speech, but in truth and action. And by this we will know that we are from the truth and will reassure our hearts before him whenever our hearts condemn us; for God is greater than our hearts, and he knows everything. (1 John 3:14-20)

That kind of language is directed against a "lovely" sentimental idea of love. It is not a question of somehow idolizing our particular human notions of love, however precious they are in our experience. We are not saying, "love is God," as though projecting a human notion onto God. Rather, "*God* is Love," in the sense that it is God who defines what love originally and ultimately means. The way God is Love is therefore disclosed in the Father's way of acting on our behalf: "God's love was revealed among us in this way: God sent his only Son into the world that we might live through him" (1 John 4:9). More precisely, "In this is love, not that we loved God but that he loved us and sent his Son to be the atoning sacrifice for our sins" (1 John 4:10). God's love remains what it is even when all human loves have run their course, have been defeated, or have even been changed into their opposite in the dark worlds of hatred and violence.

Christian life needs to be understood as a continuing progress into the full revelation of God's love. In every life there are moral ambiguities and times of perplexed conscience. But the way forward is to call on the deepest resources of the Love that enfolds our lives, inviting us to participate in the small measure of our own loving:

> There is no fear in love, but perfect love casts out fear; for fear has to do with punishment, and whoever fears has not reached perfection in love. We love because he first loved us. Those who say, 'I love God,' and hate their brothers and sisters, are liars; for those who do not love a brother or sister whom they have seen, cannot love God whom they have not seen. (1 John 4:18-20)

The conviction that God is Love must grow. It is continually tested by our practical response to our neighbor in need. "Beloved, since God loves us so much, we ought also to love one another" (1 John 4:11). Step by step, Christian life unfolds as an ever-deeper participation in the divine "Love-life." It is not as though we see more of what cannot be seen in this life. It is more a matter of becoming, step by step in the course of life, more deeply immersed in what God is: "No one has ever seen God; if we love one another, God lives in us, and his love is perfected in us" (1 John 4:12).

While we do not need to become academic theologians, each of us needs a strong "working theology" to direct our lives in the complex world of today. By reflecting on the seven key terms relevant to the confession "God is Love," we have a checklist, as it were, for both a robust theology and a genuine spirituality.

Moreover, this approach cannot but be fruitful ecumenically, since it concentrates the many considerations of Christian life on what lies at its heart. We might hope, too, that it is productive in interfaith dialogue—and in the world of dialogue in general. This overall sense of things remains a clear place to start from and return to. It is open to the depths of love and goodness evident in all communities of faith and spiritual commitment. It embraces all others in the gracious otherness of the God revealed to us in Christ. He is the Word of God incarnate amongst us (John 1:18). It is worth remembering that the first words spoken by this Word in John's Gospel is a question: "What are you looking for?" (John 1:38). In what follows, we hope to provide some way of answering that question.

CHAPTER 2

The Father: Love as Origin and End

I

In the first place, God is Love in the person of the Father, the divine source of all. The paternal originality and initiative are revealed in the clarity and conviction of John's words: "In this is love, not that we loved God but that he loved us and sent his Son" (1 John 4:10). The full meaning of adoring God as the Father will be apparent only when we have meditated on the significance of all the other terms as well. To that degree, there is a certain danger in beginning with the term "Father." We risk reducing its meaning to some cultural sense of fatherhood, whether ancient or modern, and so project onto God a cultural idol of some form. In contrast, the meaning of "our Father" is one that is revealed only through the incarnation of his Son and through his Holy Spirit dwelling within us. But that is to run ahead—and to anticipate the final self-disclosure of God when the face of the Father is revealed in the vision of God "face to face."

To identify the Father with Love means that God exists and loves as the absolute "beginning." Love precedes all creation, all time, and all human action. As the Gospel repeatedly stresses, the Father's initiative is involved in the life, action, speech, and mission of Jesus himself.[1] Because of the absolute originality and initiative of God as Love, Christians must look beyond everything that restricts or diminishes their confidence in the One who "is greater than our hearts" (1 John 3:20; see also 4:4, 18; 5:4, 9).

For Paul, too, God is invoked as Father, as primordial Love. God the Father is the original source "who has blessed us in Christ with every spiritual blessing," who has chosen us in Christ "before the foundation of the world" to be present to him in love (Eph 1:3-4). This Father is invoked and adored as the "Father of our Lord Jesus Christ" (Eph 1:2). That is to say God is *Father* in relation to the *Son*, whom he sends in order to "gather up all things in him, things in heaven and things on earth" (Eph 1:10). This "God, who is rich in mercy, out of the great love with which he loved us even when we were dead through our trespasses, made us alive together with Christ" (Eph 2:4-5). The unreserved character of Love is not defeated when it encounters its opposite—loveless inhumanity and despair: "God proves his love for us in that while we still were sinners Christ died for us" (Rom 5:8; cf. 1 John 4). The Father's love keeps on being Love and shows itself to be more intensely and unconditionally loving in its exposure to human malice and sinfulness.

The Father's love keeps on being Love not only in saving us from evil but even to the extent of inspiring the good we do, for "we are what he has made us, created in Christ Jesus for good works, which God prepared beforehand to be our way of life" (Eph 2:10). The Father is, then, the source of all we are and do, guiding us onward so that "God may be all in all" (1 Cor 15:28)—this "God and Father of all, who is above all and through all and in all" (Eph 4:6). Paul finds himself at the point of amazement and wonder: "O the depths of the riches and wisdom and knowledge of God. How unsearchable are his judgments and inscrutable his ways. . . . 'Who has given a gift to him, to receive a gift in return?'" (Rom 11:33-34).

Our adoration of the Love that God is unfolds in prayers of praise and thanksgiving to the Father, the engendering fount of trinitarian life and creative source of the worlds of nature and grace. Everything comes into being out of the sheer abundance of God's generative and creative love. There is a profound truth in speaking of God creating the universe "out of nothing." When it comes to God's creative act, nothing is first "there," as it were. But we can put that more positively by saying that God creates "out of love." All that is has been loved into being, so that at the heart of all created being is the sheer and unrestricted Love that God is. To that degree, to exist is to have been, and to continue to be, loved into being. All the goodness of the created universe is the manifestation of sheer loving on the part of God. As St. Thomas puts it, "the love of God is infusing and creating the goodness in things" (*Summa Theologica* I, q. 20, a. 2). To understand this is to recognize everything and everyone as a gift emanating from the creative Love that God is. We are what we are because of the original Love that wells up from the heart of God.

God's love presupposes no human merits. The Father's love needs no "raw material," not even good behavior on our part, to show forth his love. Love is pure gift, a sheer giving that precedes any worth, merit, or claim. Love is at the origin of our being and guides the development of all that we are. At every juncture God invites us to participate through our own action in the Love that God is:

> Beloved, let us love one another, because love is from God; everyone who loves is born of God and knows God . . . for God is love (1 John 4:7-8)

We are, therefore, not spectators but participants. Love moves us to be caught up and carried forward in a current of love-life more real than the air we breathe.

II

Love has revealed itself as coming from beyond our world and yet touching us within the time-and-space-bound limits of human existence. Sensitive religious writers try to keep a discreet reverence in their speech about God, for it is possible to talk "God" to death. Intimacy with the absolute mystery of primordial Love in the Father does not encourage religious chatter. The most genuine language is that of prayerful adoration arising from hearts intent on responding to the Love that has been given.

In some ways, "Father" as the first word of the vocabulary of Love is the most difficult. There is the danger of distortion arising from two preconceptions: the first deals with the character of God as Father, and the second is in regard to the kind of love that God is. In regard to the first, the other six terms we have listed (Son, cross, resurrection, Holy Spirit, church, and eternal life) must be

presupposed in their relation to the term "Father." The revelation
of God as Father, as the primordial Love at the origin and beginning
of everything, is the culmination of Christian faith experience. It
is important, therefore, to insist that the God of Christian faith is
invoked as Father in the matrix of all the six other terms expressive
of the Love that has been revealed.

Naming God as Father in a Christian sense does not, therefore,
begin from a generalized idea of fatherhood. It is the culmination
of a thankful experience of all the gifts of God, especially in the
sending of the Son and the Spirit. In this *eucharistia* offered to the
Father, a heartfelt thanking precedes and accompanies all thinking.
The Father is invoked out of an experience of patience, joy, and
hope. Paul encourages the Christian community even in the midst
of suffering to move forward by

> joyfully giving thanks to the Father, who has enabled you to share
> the inheritance of the saints in the light. He has rescued us from
> the power of darkness and transferred us into the kingdom of his
> beloved Son, in whom we have redemption, the forgiveness of sins.
> (Col 1:11-14)

God is thus invoked as Father only as the fulfillment of our
Christian experience. For that reason, there is a certain danger
in thinking of the Father as "the First Divine Person" in our
experience. The presumption is that we know who the Father is
apart from Christ and his Spirit. It is helpful to realize that in our
lived experience of God, the Spirit tends to come first, leading to
union with the Son in his relationship to the Father. Thus, Christian
consciousness unfolds by participating in the Son's relationship to
the One from whom he comes, in whose presence he lives, and to
whom he has returned. As sons and daughters in the Son, we are
freed to be free with God:

> For you did not receive a spirit of slavery to fall back into fear,
> but you have received a spirit of adoption. When we cry, "Abba!
> Father!" it is that very Spirit bearing witness with our spirit that
> we are children of God. (Rom 8:15-16)

God is not addressed as "lord and master" as though we were
slaves, or even "king" as though we were subjects, or even "father"

in a generalized metaphorical sense as creator of the world. For our familiar invocation of God as Father lives from the memory of Jesus' own intimate relationship with the One from whom he comes, as expressed in the words, "Abba, Father!" (Rom 8:15; cf. Mark 14:36; Matt 11:27). The Father is the One to whom Jesus is turned in the totality of his existence and from whom he possesses his deepest identity and mission.

As a result, God is named as Father in the context of Jesus' own relationship to the source of life that has begotten him and that reveals itself in him: "No one comes to the Father except through me" (John 14:6). Any attempt to go to the Father outside the way of Jesus may say a lot about human projection and fear or about the ambiguous religiosity of the human condition. But through, with, and in Jesus, the Son of the Father, God is identified as the Source of life and love: "Whoever has seen me has seen the Father" (John 14:9).

Christians, then, in union with the Son and guided by his Spirit, "dare to say" (*audemus dicere* in the old Latin liturgy), "Our Father." This is to invoke God as the Love that embraces the beginning and end of all that is.

There is another danger of distortion in speaking of God the Father. The problem is not purely intellectual. Everyone knows what fatherhood means from the physical or psychological experiences of the human family through the generations. But that obvious, natural sense of fatherhood can be an obstacle to the Christian experience of God as Father. If we begin by interpreting how God is Love merely in reference to our experience of human beings, one's idea of love can take strange turns. Our sense of the Fatherhood of God can be distorted by the cultural and psychological baggage of many kinds—as when "God" is pressed into the service of cultural patriarchy; or when God's love is reduced to a paternalistic attitude; or when our loving response takes the form of an immature dependency on an idealized parental figure.

Needless to say, there is no excuse for the extreme masculinism of much religious language. The sediment of past epochs of patriarchal experience lies thick on our present powers of expression. It tends to make us forget the subversive intimacy of Jesus' invocation of God as "Abba, Father," not to speak of the provocation inherent in his prohibition of calling anyone "father" (Matt 23:9) in the unquestioning patriarchal society of his day.

In the effort to come to some understanding of God as Love, there is no need to deal in vague notions or strange words or images. The key point of reference is the reality of supremely personal relationships. We find this notably expressed in the prayer of Jesus in chapter 17 of John's Gospel. The words of this prayer suggest a Christian self-understanding deeply connected to the "autobiographical" self-expression of God himself. Jesus prays,

> I have made your name known to those whom you gave me from the world. They were yours, and you gave them to me, and they have kept your word. Now they know that everything you have given me is from you; for the words that you gave to me I have given to them, and they have received them and know in truth that I came from you. (John 17:6-8)

The Father who expresses himself in his Word and who has sent his beloved Son into the world draws believers into the realm of new life: "And this is eternal life, that they may know you, the only true God, and Jesus Christ whom you have sent" (John 17:3). Knowing God as Father is, therefore, a dimension of eternal life itself. By taking part in God's "love-life," believers become familiar both with the divine Source and Origin and with Jesus himself, who has come into the world as the only-begotten Son. The Father is revealed as the original and sovereign Love disclosed in the world through the coming of his Son. Indeed, the Father and his Son come to dwell in those who have lovingly accepted Jesus in faith (John 14:23).

III

The statement "God is Love" first of all refers to God as "the Father" in relation to his only-begotten Son. This God is invoked as "our Father" by all who are united to Christ, the Beloved Son. The affirmation "God is Love" expresses first of all God's utterly original outpouring and initiative as the fount of all life—both within God and in the universe of divine creation. The Father is Love not merely in his gracious relationship to us, but in the eternity of his loving self-expression in the Son in the power of the Spirit. The Gospel of John presents a privileged overhearing, as it were, of the prayer of Jesus to the Father (John 17). Jesus speaks of himself as loved by the Father "before the foundation of the world" (John 17:24). The gospel keeps leading its hearers to the eternal heart of God. In a beginning before all imaginable beginnings, the Father loves his Son, who, as the Word, is the living expression of all that God is and can be for creation. Primordial, self-expressive Love is at the origin of all reality, even the reality of the divine Trinity itself.

To affirm that God is Love amounts to saying that everything derives from the divine source as a gift. All is given and is to be received in the unfolding of time, as "the gift of God" (John 4:10). God is Love and gives as the absolute "beginning." This self-giving love precedes all creation, all time, and all human action, enfolds all becoming, and is the end of all fulfillments. The recognition of this primordial love precedes all human response: "In this is love, not that we loved God but that he loved us and sent his Son" (1 John 4:10).

The conception of God as Love belongs to the innermost depths of God's eternal life. The Gospel of John, for instance, repeatedly stresses that the Father acts as the generative initiative involved in the life, action, speech, and mission of Jesus himself.[2]

When God as Father "so loved the world that he gave his only Son" (John 3:16) to offer the gift of eternal life, he was acting in character. The Father gives what is most intimately his own—"his only Son"—into the region of the utterly other ("the world"). Not only is the world separate from the Father; it is also alienated from him because of our sins. When that all-originating Love finds us in our lovelessness, we can respond in kind: "We love because he first loved us" (1 John 4:19).

When we are drawn toward the infinite, all-generous mystery, faith cannot be determined by sacred sites or ethnic loyalties: "You will worship the Father neither on this mountain nor in Jerusalem" (John 4:21). God is beyond all the limits and boundaries the world imposes: "If you knew the gift of God . . ." (John 4:10). The greatness of the gift prevents us from associating our relationship with the Father too easily with the natural or cultural conditions of our existence. We must avoid the temptation to bottle the new wine of our relationship with the Father in old—or new—containers.

Despite the modern psychological ambivalence in regard to "father images," along with the feminist criticism of the long history of patriarchy, "Father" in its Christian meaning denotes the primordial and prodigal character of God's love and the freedom in which it acts. We are not dealing with God in an automatic fashion but, as receivers of a pure gift, as the "beloved" in the embrace of the God who is Love. The love that has brought forth the whole of creation, holds it in existence, and guides its emergence at every stage is revealed as Love that has from the beginning destined us to share in its divine life.

IV

This understanding of "God is Love" counters the idolization of God as a patriarchal power. It also undermines any suspicion of God's unimaginably prodigal love as being capricious in some way. When the Creed, for instance, speaks of "the Father Almighty" (*omnipotens, pantokrator*), it means first of all that there is no other beginning more radical than God's creative and self-giving love. The whole of history unfolds from this original Love in ways that surpass all expectation and imagination:

> Now to him who by the power at work within us is able to accomplish abundantly far more than all we can ask or imagine, to him be glory in the church and in Christ Jesus to all generations, forever and ever. Amen. (Eph 3:20-21)

Hence, the Father is "almighty" precisely in the power of his love—to give, to create, and to transform. And yet there is a divine reserve in evidence. The Father refuses to appear in our world except in the form of the self-giving love that his Son embodies. In Christ both "the power of God and the wisdom of God" (1 Cor 1:24) are shown forth.

There is a further point. The "almighty" character of the Father's love means that God can communicate in a way that is beyond the many kinds of giving found in creation. In the finite human world, we enter relationships, express our feelings and intentions in a huge variety of symbols, and "put ourselves into" loving activities in various ways. Yet even in our most generous and outgoing acts, we have to acknowledge limits. There is a point beyond which our kind of loving becomes tragic. It can end in being either self-destructive for ourselves or oppressive of the other—or, more likely, both. Not to accept inherent limits on time, energy, and personal capacity is to have only a tired, exhausted shell of one's self to offer to others. More tragically still, if any of us pretends to a quasi-almighty loving of the other and tries to enter into their very being and become their total life, then a destructive, oppressive possessiveness is the dismal result. If we attempt to love beyond our human limits, we are diminished in who we are and oppress those we pretend to love.

In contrast, the Father is "almighty" in his loving, unconstrained by any finite limits. As the source of the creative Word and the Spirit, he alone is inexhaustibly life-giving in love. His love is unreserved, and the Love that he is works in the mind and in the heart and through the whole of creation to give us our true selves—intelligent, free creatures capable of loving others. In other words, the Father is not lessened by what he gives, nor does he diminish those who receive it.

One result of God's special love is that it is able to both respect and enhance human freedom. Divine freedom is not a rival compared to human freedom but is its creative source, ever working to enlarge and fulfill our liberty. The limitless love of the Father, in the words of the prophet, plucks out "the heart of stone" and replaces it with "a heart of flesh" (Ezek 36:26). The greater our freedom, the more creative our liberty and the more the love of the Father is revealed and delights in our flourishing.

Still, the power of Love is revealed in its patience and respect for the shape and dynamisms of the created world. Love has had time and has made space for us in the billions of years needed for the unfolding of our universe. Dante wrote of the "the love that moves the sun and the other stars" (*l'amor che muove il sole e le altre stelle*). Today, we can think of that Love creating and moving the universe from the first moment of the big bang to the formation of the galaxies and the stars—as well as the planets and, finally, our earth. There followed the emergence of primitive life three and a half billion years ago until it reached human life itself, through which the universe became aware of itself in the consciousness of the human mind and heart as a gift of limitless wonder. Love has time for the whole of human history to grow to its own grandeur and scope.

Nor are the "almighty" ways of Love defeated by human evil. Though Love is patient, it is not endlessly frustrated or held in reserve. As we will see, in raising up the Crucified, the power of

Love breaks out and shows itself in an irreversible event. Love comes to its own triumph over death and evil. But it works through the inexhaustible imagination of Love. It does not crowd human freedom but allows for and calls forth the freedom of our faith, hope, and charity. The Father is almighty and his love is omnipotent. It is in no way constrained by human limitations or resistance—even those resulting from our own guilt and incapacity:

> And by this we know we are from the truth and will reassure our hearts before him whenever our hearts condemn us; for God is greater than our hearts, and he knows everything. (1 John 3:19-20)

And so God is the loving source of life and existence, preceding anything we are or do. Our existence in the first place is an uncanny gift; but there is a further unimaginable realm of life and being that can come to us only if we receive it as a gift—as the grace of God. When faith is open to the Love that is the inexhaustible source of all giving, human limits are not the determining factor: "All things can be done for the one who believes" (Mark 9:23). What seems impossible for the human heart in its longing for the eternities of life and love and universal communion is not impossible for the all-powerful love of God at work through the universe: "For mortals it is impossible, but not for God; for God all things are possible" (Mark 10:27). Nothing and no one is outside the reach of this Love. What we most love and fear to lose is not left to the mercy of what we most dread, but is kept within the impossible possibilities of God: "We know that all things work together for good for those who love God, who are called according to his purpose" (Rom 8:28). Faith is being open to what Love can do, will do, and is doing throughout the whole of creation. Admittedly, the totality of what is in the making cannot be known to us. It must be left to the limitless possibilities of Love operating in God's way and in God's time.

Love is not blocked by the power of evil, as though what is worst in our experience determines forever the way things will be. Nor is Love changed into vengeance by the machinations of malice, even when human sin crucifies the Beloved Son himself. Love does not descend to the level of lovelessness and violence. The Father refuses to act in any way other than being the source of mercy and forgiveness and so breaking the vicious circle of revenge and hatred.

It moves countless children of God to risk being "merciful, just as your Father is merciful" (Luke 6:36). Love, seemingly defenseless in the real world, is the ultimately victorious power, despite the conflicts and quandaries inherent in all our lives:

> No, in all these things we are more than conquerors through him who loved us. For I am convinced that neither death, nor life, nor angels, nor rulers, nor things present, nor things to come, nor powers, nor height, nor depth, nor anything else in all creation, will be able to separate us from the love of God in Christ Jesus our Lord. (Rom 8:37-39)

In the guise of a humble and vulnerable love, the almighty Father exemplifies the quality that Jesus demands of the disciples, the "true greatness" that is prepared to take the last place in this world (cf. Mark 9:36). Yet it alone can topple the idols constructed out of human pride and greed, which have demanded so much human sacrifice. The Father, the Almighty, the God who is Love, acts to subvert selfishness and violence. Love alone disarms our hearts and opens the way of true wisdom: "God's foolishness is wiser than human wisdom, and God's weakness is stronger than human strength" (1 Cor 1:25).

By praying to "our Father," we share in God's almighty love and so share in what God is doing in the universe. Prayer may seem to be a powerless activity, but it draws on the energies of Love to heal and transform. It is not as though God is made more loving by our prayers. It is more that the prodigality of God's love inspires those who pray to take part in the great act of God's continuing love for all creation.

Early in the second century during the reign of Emperor Trajan, Ignatius, bishop of Antioch, was escorted to Rome for execution. His journey ended when he was thrown to wild beasts, most probably in the Colosseum. On his way, however, he felt that he was on another kind of journey. The martyr, later described by St. John Chrysostom as "a soul seething with the divine desire,"[3] declared, "There is living water in me, which speaks and says inside me, 'Come to the Father!'"[4]

God is the end of the journey. The path of Israel through history moves into a holy darkness—what a later mystical writer called "the cloud of unknowing." It is the darkness of mystery suggested in Israel's invocation of God as Yʜᴡʜ—which, in one of its many possible translations, can mean not only "I ᴀᴍ ᴡʜᴏ I ᴀᴍ" but also "I ᴡɪʟʟ ʙᴇ ᴡʜᴏ I ᴡɪʟʟ ʙᴇ" (Exod 3:14). Those who follow the way of God move forward only through surrender and trust. The words of the First Letter of John sum up this tradition of holy darkness: "No one has ever seen God; if we love one another, God lives in us, and his love is perfected in us" (1 John 4:12). This draws on the message of John's Gospel: "No one has ever seen God. It is God the only Son, who is close to the Father's heart, who has made him known" (John 1:18). The "invisibility" of the Father is further underlined in the words of Jesus: "Not that anyone has seen the Father except the one who is from God; he has seen the Father" (John 6:46). Admittedly, in relation to this God, we are dealing with what cannot be fully known within the limits of human knowledge: "No one has ever seen God" (John 1:18; 1 John 4:12). However, through faith in Christ we become personally familiar with the mystery and participate in it: "It is God the only Son, who is close to the Father's heart, who has made him known" (John 1:18).

Some of the world's greatest philosophers and thinkers, all the way from Heraclitus to Hegel, Marx, Freud, and Heidegger, have taken for granted that the conflict and the violence of endless competition are woven into the fundamental fabric of the universe. In the kingdom of the Father, things are different. The texture of the universe is determined by its being the Father's creation held together in the divine Word (John 1:3, 10). Creation is being drawn into a God-given destiny. Our hope is to enter into that communion of life and love that unites the Father and the Son: "As you, Father, are in me and I am in you, may they also be in us" (John 17:21). As it moves more deeply into this great communion of life and love, Christian consciousness is ever expanding. Its source, measure, and goal is the Father himself: "Beloved, let us love one another, because love is from God; everyone who loves is born of God and knows God . . . for God is love" (1 John 4:7-8). Christian consciousness thus expands in a divine milieu of unity and communion (see John 17:21-23). A New Testament witness "from the beginning" writes in terms of life and light: "We declare to you the eternal life that

was with the Father and was revealed to us" (1 John 1:2). Even
the dark, loveless world of selfishness and violence is flooded with
light: "God is light and in him there is no darkness at all" (1 John
1:5). This light shines into all our relationships: "Whoever loves a
brother or sister lives in the light, and in such a person there is no
cause for stumbling" (1 John 2:10).

While there is no darkness in God, evil casts long shadows in
the history of Christian conduct. We would all like to claim that
we have lived so radiantly in the Light that God's all-embracing
love shines out through our lives. But it is no good to pretend to
love God when our love for our neighbor falls short: "Those who
do not love a brother or sister whom they have seen, cannot love
God whom they have not seen" (1 John 4:20). The implication
is that only in an other-directed, social way of life can believers
know the Father. To pray and to work that the will of our Father
"be done on earth as it is in heaven" is in stark contrast with the
fabrications of private fantasy. The name of "Father" does not spring
from a private psycho-mythology but occurs, rather, in the context
of socially responsible and compassionate communication. Ideally,
it inspires an outgoing, generous, and loving way of life. Doing the
will of our Father in heaven powerfully affects our way of inhabiting
and shaping the world of the present.

John sums it up: "Those who say, 'I love God,' and hate their
brothers and sisters, are liars" (1 John 4:20). If religion becomes
an excuse on the part of some for not forgiving, for not being open
to the whole world as the object of God's love, then the question
arises as to who their "god" is and whose "children" they might be. If
religious conduct leads to hatred and the violent exclusion of others
in God's name, then what "god" are we talking about? If our basic
motivations are making a big name for ourselves in this world rather
than hallowing the name of "our Father," a fundamental distortion
has entered our existence. Fortunately, in the remarkable, gently
consoling words of the First Letter of John, even if "our hearts
condemn us . . . God is greater than our hearts" (1 John 3:20).
But there is bracing advice as well in the concluding words, "Little
children, keep yourselves from idols" (1 John 5:21).

Turning to the Father as the infinite source of creative love is
a quality of the life of grace. It inspires in all our being and acting
an experience of the sheer gift and power of giving that emanates

from God. In that sense, the divine gift undermines any pretense of a self-contained existence as if it were the product of one's own designs. There is infinitely more going on than our self-referential plans and projects recognize. God acts before we act—and in all our action. In the cosmic perspective, the generative love of God is eternally active, before the birth of this temporal universe and in every phase of its emergence. It was in action before any of us were born. It is there too in our deaths, when all mortal beings must come to the end of their powers of acting and face the ending of this present mode of being. Hence, the generosity of God as incalculable source is at the beginning and the end of all existence, as well as in every moment in between.

Every *now* is charged with the unstinted and incalculable creativity of the Father's love. The God who made everything out of nothing can surely, with the inexhaustible power of Love, bring what we are to its fulfillment. What is required of us as children of God is surrender to the scope and sway of Love, in life and in death. Faith means, then, surrender to Love as the ultimate truth at the heart of all existence. Hope means committing oneself to the future determined finally only by such Love. Through charity we are conformed to the utter generosity of God's self-giving.

VI

Because of the absolute initiative of the Father's love, Christian hope must reach forward, beyond everything that restricts or diminishes its confidence, to the One who "is greater than our hearts" (1 John 3:20). The horizon of Christian hope expands when neither the gift nor the giving nor the giver are subject to any limits. The future opens up as a realm of the love whose source, measure, and goal is the Father himself: "Beloved, let us love one another, because love is from God; everyone who loves is born of God and knows God . . . for God is love" (1 John 4:7-8). Hope relies on the power of Jesus' prayer: "As you, Father, are in me and I am in you, may they also be in us, so that the world may believe that you have sent me" (John 17:21). His prayer continues, "so that they may be one, as we are one, I in them and you in me, that they become completely one" (vv. 22-23). John writes of himself as a witness "from the beginning"

(1 John 1:1). He relates these dimensions of love and unity to the experience of life and light: "We declare to you the eternal life that was with the Father and was revealed to us" (1 John 1:2). As a result, "Whoever loves a brother or sister lives in the light, and in such a person there is no cause for stumbling" (1 John 2:10).

Yet there may be a cause for stumbling from other sources. While God is Light, evil is the zone of the photophobic, of those who flee the light and hide in darkness. We must all confess that there are dark corners in our hearts and in our world at large. The usual list includes racism, sexism, imperialism, patriarchalism, unbridled capitalism, and bigotry in all its forms. These forms of inhumanity have one thing in common: they are causes of stumbling for others who are made to feel that they do not belong to the family of God.

We briefly return to one problem already mentioned. It is connected to the frustrating limitations of language and the limits of translation, as in the English use of the word "father" and the repetition of the masculine personal pronoun in that context. The feminist critique of cultural communication has opened the way to a more inclusive sense of humanity and a proper recognition of the dignity, role, and giftedness of women. This is a matter of historic significance. I consider, however, that its importance is diminished if it is reduced to the problems inherent in the English language. The true scandal consists not in the deficiencies of a written language but in a lack of respect in living communication. That would indicate an unjust and unloving community. If that were the case, failure lies in not adoring the Father "in spirit and truth" but insisting on some lesser, other, self-regarding measure.

In this connection, it is worth noting that while Jesus reveals the Father as his Son and Word, Mary as the Mother of God, the mother of this Son, reveals an aspect of the generative Love that God is. The Father, while remaining hidden to human sight, declares that Jesus is his Son, the Beloved, and commands the disciples to listen to him. Likewise, Mary remains largely hidden in the life of Jesus. However, as the first of believers, she tells his followers, "Do whatever he tells you" (cf. John 2:5). From the cross, Jesus declares Mary mother of the Beloved Disciple. In such ways the Fatherhood of God is represented by the Motherhood of Mary.

This is to say that Mary figures as an icon of the Father. In the sword that pierces her heart, in the request she makes of her Son, in the silent love of her life, in her standing at the cross, she embodies the patient, life-giving love of the Father. For the generations that have addressed her as mother, she expresses the tenderness of the Father who has given what is most intimately his own for our sake. She brings forth in time the One whom the Father eternally begets. She acts in the power of the Spirit, with which the Father acts, to give her son for the world's salvation. Against the distortions of religious fantasy, Mary embodies a corrective to any excessive masculinization of the divine.

In the light and energy of the Father's love, forgiveness received by anyone must show itself in forgiveness of others. Any judgment on the moral status of others or their worth in the sight of God must yield to the incalculable dimensions of God's self-giving love. It follows that a Christian judgment on the world or this present age cannot be totally negative. Our relative judgments must, of course, be made—but not so as to be made outside the domain of a boundless mercy. The ever-greater mystery is always Love, not evil. The universe of grace allows no meritocracy. To receive God's mercy is to be left with nothing but God. There is nothing to cling to—not even one's sinfulness—as an excuse for holding back from surrendering to an ever-greater love. When Love is understood as mercy, Christian conscience is freed from the dead weight of the past with its hopeless burden of self-justification and blame. "Be merciful, just as your Father is merciful" (Luke 6:36). All are summoned to enter humbly into the merciful universe of *our* Father.

CHAPTER 3

The Son: Love as Self-Giving

 In *so* loving the world, the Father is Love, engendering and expressing itself. In giving his only Son, Love is uniquely self-giving by giving what is most intimate to itself. This uniquely intimate and unreserved communication is summed up in the Johannine statement "For God so loved the world that he gave his only Son" (John 3:16). The Father's giving of his only Son marks the extent of his involvement in so loving the world. It shows how God puts himself into the work of loving the world into life. So intimately related is the Son to the Father's own self that the First Letter of John can state, "No one who denies the Son has the Father; everyone who confesses the Son has the Father also" (1 John 2:23).

In order to appreciate the reality of God's love and the gift that has occurred in the coming of the Son into the world, the mind of faith had to expand to take in a hitherto unimaginable reality. And the language of faith had to learn new terms if it were to appreciate the unique divine communication that had taken place. The early councils of the church had to tussle with the problem. They

26

had to find the best way of formulating what faith meant when it confessed Jesus as truly Son of the Father and, indeed, truly our human brother.

Part of the problem was that the one God of Israel and of Christian faith was now revealed to be "one" in a way not previously imagined. With the coming of Jesus and the sending of the Spirit, the reality of the one living God came to be understood as a communion existing between the Father with the Son in the unity of the Holy Spirit. This implied that the Son is not to be confused with the Father but is truly divine in relation to the Father and, like the Father, deserving of the divine worship.

Theological problems and language difficulties aside, the Father's giving his only Son for the world's salvation remains always an immense mystery of the love that outstrips all human categories. The divine character of God's gift is clearly evident in the New Testament:

> Long ago God spoke to our ancestors in many and various ways by the prophets, but in these last days he has spoken to us by a Son, whom he appointed heir of all things, through whom he also created the worlds. He is the reflection of God's glory and the exact imprint of God's very being, and he sustains all things by his powerful word. (Heb 1:1-3)

In this passage and in numerous others, the Son possesses a divine status. He is not a human being somehow adopted by a divine parent; nor is he to be confused with the Father from whom he comes. Rather, he relates to the Father—and to the world—in his own right, a divine Someone in relation to the Father and to us.

To speak, then, of the Son of God is to add an unimaginable personal dimension to how God is Love. The terms that follow (cross, resurrection, Holy Spirit, church, and eternal life) more fully display what divine Sonship means. At the moment, we will concentrate on what is meant when faith speaks of the love of God in terms of the Son who was given for the life of the world. The fundamental point is this: the God of love is uniquely self-giving because God has such a self to give—a self whose whole being is to give and to love. In the eternal being of God, the Father is Love by communicating himself to the Other, his Son and Word. In the realm of time and space, the Father gives into the world what is most intimately his own, the Son, as "God from God, Light from Light."

Three things follow. First, the way God gives limitlessly exceeds all human and created forms of self-giving. By sending his Son, the Father has not just done *something* for us, but expresses himself through this divine *Someone*, the Son and Word. Just as the Father communicates all that he is *to* the Son, he can express all that he is *through* this Son sent into the world.

Second, when we speak of the Son of God, it means that God, as the Father, is never alone and never not giving of himself to the Other. He is not alone, since there is the beloved Other to whom he has communicated his divine being. His love is never sterile, because he is eternally generating the Son and, in him, expressing all the infinite possibilities of creation.

Third, though God is revealed in every aspect of creation, he is fully and uniquely expressed only in his beloved, only-begotten Son. God is Love eternally. The infinite source of life engenders an Other and eternally communicates itself. Faith expands when it recognizes the depth and extent of the divine vitality and its unique capacity to give.

By sending his Son into the world, the Father, as Love, is reaching out to the world of creation. And so, the mission of Jesus is to draw all into the communion of love and life that exists between the Father and the Son. The aim of the Son is to enfold all who follow him into the eternal life of God (see John 17:20-24). To believe in him is to be in communion "with the Father and with his Son Jesus Christ" (1 John 1:3). Faith experiences the Love that God is by acknowledging that the Son is the unique self-expression and self-gift of the Father: "God's love was revealed among us in this way: God sent his only Son into the world so that we might live through him" (1 John 4:9). Christian existence, therefore, finds its focus in the unreserved, personal self-communication of God to the world. It is a form of self-giving and self-expression so radical that it is possible only to God. The Word, who is what God is, is made flesh and so enters into the conversation of human history.

II

The New Testament interprets the history of God's dealing with creation as culminating in the coming of the Son among us. God has created this universe in space and time to achieve a divine purpose.

Indeed, time itself is held together and directed to its end by the Son in his timeless genesis in the depth of divine life. His coming forth is a dynamism reaching into every moment of history. In terms of physical laws, entropy follows on the passing of time and so works to diminish events of even the greatest significance. But the eternal vitality of God present in every moment continuously renews creation: every instant, every *now*, is filled with the liveliness of God's self-giving love. There is no time in which God is not the Living One, eternally begetting the Son out of love. This is to say that the identity of Jesus as Son flows from his being eternally begotten of the Father. His identity is not defined by time; it defines and shapes time. In that perspective, time is pregnant with divine meaning and direction. It is no longer a pointless succession of events slowly winding down as the forces of entropy gain control. The flow of time is powered by the generation that takes place within God. Time becomes the carrier not only of earthly life as we know it but also of the promise of unending life that flows from the divine life itself; each moment is filled with a God-given vitality.

Through the incarnation of the eternal Son, time is radically personalized. It flows on as stream bearing divine gifts. In the deepest sense, God "has time" for the world's unfolding. Our fragmented experience of time and history finds its coherence and direction in the identity of Jesus, the only Son of the Father. When the Word becomes flesh, God becomes what is "other" in the extreme so that all created "others" can be enfolded into God's own life. Indeed, everything disclosed in the birth, life, death, and resurrection of the Son is tied back into the depths of the divine reality itself. Who Jesus is in time is identical with who he is before all ages, in the eternal life of God.

In the words of the Creed, the Son is "the Only Begotten Son of God." One of the earliest and most challenging heresies is associated with the name of Arius of Alexandria. Arius maintained that God was necessarily alone. If God is God, there can be no Other within the divine life. God cannot share his divine life and being. Any "other" coming forth from God had to be less than God and therefore "made" by the solitary, supreme Maker and thus had to be part of creation. The Son, then, had to be located on the side of creation—even if ranked as the highest of creatures. Behind Arius's thinking was the Greek philosophical notion of the solitary, transcendent God—who, naturally, was not and could not be self-giving, since God was not a giving self. That defied the philosophical imagination; it suggested that God, by loving in this supremely self-giving way, would be acting against his own divine nature.

The church's response was quite the opposite. It came to see clearly that for God to communicate himself to this Other, it would not mean that God would be acting against the divine nature. It would mean, rather, in the Christian understanding of what God is like, that such a personal communication belonged to the innermost essence of the God who had been revealed in Christ. In its response, then, to Arius, the Council of Nicaea (325) appealed not to the philosophical remote and solitary "god" of Greek philosophy but to the biblical experience of God—the God who lives and acts by communicating his innermost being. That would lead eventually to a deep understanding of God as the Trinity, with the three Divine Persons mutually related in the one divine life of communion. The God of Christian faith is, therefore, the God of inmost eternal self-communication. God is Love, and that Love is self-giving because that is how God is.

To affirm that the Son is "begotten, not made" is to rule out any sense of his being a temporal creation. In the eternal flow of divine life, Love engenders its perfect self-expression within the timeless depths of God. Yet Love holds in its heart the intention to create the universe in time. It thereby intends to form the world in which the Word can become flesh and in which the Son can be a human being with us in order to draw humankind into the life of God.

When the Father's love brings forth the Son, he is "Light from Light." So much does the Light express its perfect image in the Other that the Son is himself a source of light, not merely its reflection or a created mirror (cf. John 8:12; Luke 2:32). God is Light and the Son is Light because God is Love. Faith lives in the love-light in which heart and mind expand in the life of God. In this regard, the Son is not just a human symbol of the divine or a way of speaking imaginatively about human destiny and our connection with God. Rather, Jesus, as Son, is the self-expression of God in a manner that makes clear what the love of God actually means: "God is light and in him there is no darkness at all" (1 John 1:5).

The Son, who is truly God, comes forth from the true God. But the mode of his coming forth is not like the production of anything created: he is not "made." Rather, he is eternally "begotten" in the self-giving that belongs to the life of God. The Son is the Other into whom the Father has lovingly poured the fullness of being, so that he receives everything from the Father. But in this relationship of giving and receiving, the Son is not less than the Father. The trinitarian communication implies no diminishment or neediness on the part of the Divine Persons. We cannot think of the Son apart from his receiving all from the Father. Likewise, we cannot think of the Father save in relation to the Son, as eternally communicating his godhead to the Son.

Hence, Love communicates nothing less than itself: the Son is "consubstantial" with the Father. It follows that the original activity of God is not that of creating the universe but that of a life of eternal self-giving. The Son is God from God, Light from Light, and Love from Love. In this, the Father communicates the fullness of divine being to the Son. And from this original self-communication, all the gifts of God flow into creation.

As "consubstantial," the Son uniquely reveals what the Father is. Through God's self-expression in the Son, faith comes to an intimate and personal knowledge of what God is like. In other words, in Christian experience "God" is not primarily a big religious idea but is the infinite Love that has disclosed itself through the Word made flesh. "Our Lord Jesus Christ" is the living definition of what God means. All other ideas pale in comparison with the Father's own self-expression in Christ. Admittedly, faith can lose its focus—as happened in the case of Arius. He asserted that Christ as Son and Word *had* to be created because what was truly "divine" could not originate from another, nor become incarnate, nor suffer as a human being. Therefore, Christ had to be a creature, and the Son has to have a temporal beginning. In other words, God could not be self-giving in this way. This limited perspective allowed that although the Father has acted and performed a great *something* for our salvation, he had not given a divine *Someone* to be our savior—his beloved Son, his divine, eternal, and coequal "Other."

The Father's generation of the Son is the primordial movement in the life of the Trinity. It shows that there is an "Other" in God. Further, it throws light on how we understand the "otherness" of creation in relation to God, the Creator. When Love's capacity to "other" itself is essential to the divine life, we begin to understand the creativity of divine freedom in summoning the universe into being. In this perspective, the divine "fathering" of the Son is the eternal presupposition to all divine making. That is to say that the existence of all creation, and of each one of us in that creation, is first of all conceived in the eternal Word and Son. That timeless generation bears further fruit in time. And in time it is recognized when faith confesses both that the Son is "begotten, not made" and that "through him all things were made." Creation is, as it were, a temporal extension of the generation of the Son and the expression of the divine Word: "all things came into being through him" (John 1:3).

Contemporary science is increasingly familiar with how the cosmos is a totality of interconnected events in the great emergent process of the universe. The hologram, rather than the mechanism of the clock, most symbolizes our present sense of reality. Each element of the universe is part of a whole and participates in that interconnected totality. For its part, faith affirms that primordial agency of the Father and the all-inclusive meaning of God's creative Word. There is a basic consistency and radical direction in all that is. The Father is creator of all, and this *all* is made through him, our Lord Jesus Christ, the only Son. "[A]ll things were made"—and are being made—through the Word, the divine self-expression. In him occurs that original "fathering forth" of the Son as the original and final form of the world's being and becoming.

In contemplating Christ, faith perceives the universe of things, processes, and persons as conceived through the eternal self-expression of God in the Word. In that infinite light, the Father knows and loves the Son and the whole of creation in him. This coherence of all in Christ makes the universe, in its every element, energy, and level of consciousness, radically interrelated. At the core of all reality is the supreme relationship that Christ personifies: he is totally from and for the Father in the Spirit of Love. Consequently, he is unreservedly "for us men and for our salvation." He communicates faith's specific field of awareness of God in all things, and of all things in God. The trinitarian relationships that make God divine also underpin the reality of the created world. To exist is to be related to the other—to be ecstatic, drawn out of ourselves, to live and die into the ultimately holy, the wholeness of God's creation in Christ.

III

Faith in the universe created in Christ does not permit believers to exclude anyone or anything from the realm of God's love. Nothing and no one can be shut out from the promise of life. Again, the elegance of a beautiful vision is not the issue here. Nor is it a matter simply of cultivating an optimistic outlook. The challenge consists, rather, in actually following Christ as the Way, in the energies of love and hope. In Christ, whatever the scandal of our separations and enmities in this present time, faith becomes hope that we will all belong ultimately together.

The way of Christ does not disrupt creation or put believers into conflict with it. To believe is to dwell in creation in its unique coherence in Christ: "In him all things hold together" (Col 1:17). Creation is unified in Christ in a radically original manner: "All things came into being through him, and without him not one thing came into being" (John 1:3).

The Word made flesh is the great poem of the almighty Poet, the Maker of all things. In the human existence of Jesus the divine Artist expresses the Word of life in the world. We affirm "God is Love" because in Christ God is self-expressed. In him all humanity finds its fulfillment and ultimate blessing in God. The reality of this love means that Jesus is neither a Divine Person hiding behind a human face nor a human person adopted into a divine sphere. He is God truly among us, God rendered invocable, God expressed and available to the eyes and ears and touch and taste of faith. In a way that neither reduces God nor destroys our humanness, the infinite distance between God and creation is bridged. Jesus Christ is truly God and truly human. In this sense he is "the man," the Human One, the ultimate form of the humanity that Love is bringing forth.

The human name of the Son is "Jesus." The fact that he bears a particular, though very common, name underscores the reality of the incarnation. The Word of God is uniquely embodied in him. Jesus is a person in human history, located geographically in a particular region, speaking and spoken to in a particular language and in the context of a particular culture and political situation. The name of Jesus serves to remind faith of its origins in history. For Christian faith is not primarily based on a principle of thought or action, or even on inspired writings, but on a person: a historically identifiable "he," a "you" who can call us each by name even as we address him. Christian faith means living a relationship with this God-given, humanly named Other. Whatever the overwhelming glory of God, we reach to its heart in meeting such a person with such a name:

> Then a cloud overshadowed them, and from the cloud there came a voice, "This is my Son, the Beloved; listen to him!" Suddenly when they looked around, they saw no one with them any more, but only Jesus. (Mark 9:7-8)

God has chosen to become present personally to creation. The infinite mystery subjects itself to the limits and struggles of earthly human existence. In Christ, God is compassionately involved on the inside of this whole groaning totality of the universe. That kind of immersion in time and space will take the Son to the cross, to burial among the dead, to the descent into hell (as the Apostles' Creed has it). Through Christ, Love reaches into what we most dread—the realm of defeat, failure, hopelessness. Love pours itself out and expresses itself in the self-emptying of the Son:

> Though he was in the form of God, [he] did not regard equality with God as something to be exploited, but emptied himself, taking the form of a slave, being born in human likeness. And being found in human form, he humbled himself and became obedient to the point of death—even death upon a cross. (Phil 2:6-8)

IV

The Son, the Light from Light and true God from true God, now lives out his relationship to the Father from within creation. Because he took flesh and lived a human existence, God is revealed as a limitless compassion enfolding that creation to itself. Past classical times envisaged reality as a great ladder of being. God was above, the uppermost reality, holding the great ladder of being upright—with God above and the earth below. Such a sense of reality suggested metaphors of ascent and descent in the way God was present to creation; God comes down so that we might go up.

Today, with an evolutionary model of thought, given the brilliant explorations that have probed into the cosmic history of the universe as it emerges through billions of years from the big bang to the present moment, reality is imagined as a stupendous, ever-expanding fertile process. The accent now is less on an upward and downward vertical movement on a ladder of being. The emphasis today is more on the horizontal, on what is coming to be, on the interconnected emergence of everything in the great universal process.

And so, for the Father to send his Son in the incarnation, it is less a matter of the Son "coming down" from heaven or being sent "from above." It suggests more the divine act by which the Son, present to all things and in whom all things are made, emerges from the innermost depths of reality where God dwells and acts. The mystery hidden behind and in the emergence of the cosmos now comes forth within it. The Father gives his Son as the catalyst of the final stage of what is coming to be. The Word is incarnate in living flesh within the cosmos. Life, in a new and final form, has appeared to draw all to itself. As the offer of a new and final becoming for the world, the Son is now present within the process of the world's becoming. He is no longer outside or beyond, but within the actual world that is coming to be. When the Son is one of us, God is present to the world in a new way. Inextinguishable light now shines in the huge darkness of space and time; the reality of ultimate Love is enfleshed there. In the Word's becoming flesh, the flesh of creation is opened to its final destiny.

Love sends the Son into the world to find its expression in the incarnation of the Word. It so takes place that neither the reality of God nor the reality of creation is diminished. The divine reality is revealed for what it is—Love giving itself into the limitation and darkness of creation's freedom and independence. On the other hand, the integrity of creation is respected. Love comes to creation as it is and to human beings as they are. There is no fusion of the divine and the human into some hybrid existence, which would undermine the truth of both. Jesus Christ is not a centaur, an actor in a mythology of love, belonging neither to the divine nor the human realm. The classic attempt to articulate a grammar designed to respect the realism of God's self-gift in Christ and the genuine humanness of Jesus is found in the words of the Council of Chalcedon of AD 451:

> One and the same Son, Our Lord Jesus Christ, the same perfect in divinity and perfect in humanity, the same truly God, . . . the same one in being with the Father as to his divinity.[1]

In the language of this classic doctrine, Jesus Christ, even while being one of us in a completely human way, remains one with God as the divine self-expression. The divine realm of being and relationship and the human realm of belonging and becoming are not to be confused, for there remain

> two natures without confusion or change, without division or separation, the distinction of the natures not being abolished by the union, but on the contrary, the properties of each nature remaining intact, and coming together in the one person or subject, not by being split or divided into two persons, but one only unique Son, God, Word, Lord Jesus Christ.[2]

When infinite Love seeks to express itself to creation, the human is created to receive it. We are *here* in order to receive the Gift and to glorify the Giver. Consequently, the incarnation does not imply that the human is invaded by the divine as by some foreign subjugating power. In Christ, human existence finds its most complete meaning and fulfillment. To be human is to be open to the infinite. It demands searching for ultimate meaning in a history of patient pursuit of truth and longing for the absolute good. As the self-gift of Love, the incarnation is the fulfillment of seemingly unfulfillable human longings.

The incarnation is the event by which Love's will for human beings is realized. The human capacity for God is no longer an unrealizable possibility but is something already actualized in the existence of Jesus Christ. The presence that secretly powered all the world's becoming over its billions of years, that energized the dynamics of its complex material organization and development, and that presided over the emergence of life and the dawning of consciousness was the Love that was to declare itself in Christ. It worked in the struggles and creativity of human history and in the long wait for the mystery to reveal itself. Finally, it was disclosed when the Word became flesh. In him, the divine reality is revealed as loving creativity continually calling forth a response on our part. The incarnation in this way affirms both what God is and what we are—God as self-expressive Love and human beings as "so loved" (John 3:16). The divine is not a threat to our humanity; rather, it is the space in which our humanity is fully realized.

The incarnation is an expanding event. It unfolds in the drama of human and cosmic history. The Word has entered into the whole process of human becoming, within the total event of the emergence of the universe. Jesus is born, grows, awakes to human consciousness, speaks human words, communicates with fellow human beings, and receives into his mind and imagination the varied beauty of creation. He knows human weakness and human temptation. He is at the mercy of others for good and for ill. He suffers the price of freedom in the path he chooses. He is condemned and crucified; he dies and is buried. All this is involved in the incarnation. Furthermore, in his resurrection and ascension he becomes the promise of a new humanity in a transformed creation.

In this larger sense, the incarnation is a continuing event. It will not be complete until the Love he embodies, the cause he lived for, and the Spirit he breathes finally include all who will come to call him "brother." The incarnation expands in all members of his Body. It unfolds until he is clothed with the whole of creation and that creation is itself transformed in the glory of his risen life.

Christian experience of God's love is not focused primarily in a doctrine or a theory, or in a theology or a philosophy, or even in a creed or a holy book, or in an idea or an ideal. It turns on a relationship to this One who breathed the air of this planet with us and who, risen from the dead, remains present in our midst. He is still a human being, marked with the wounds of living among us. He nourishes his followers with Love's most elemental symbols in the bread and wine of the Eucharist. When from the heart of faith we invoke him as "You," we find in him the meaning of God, ourselves, and the whole universe. Neither "God" nor "humanity" can ever mean the same again. God has been revealed; and humanity is reshaped by the Love that has come into the world.

The extent of this Love is further disclosed through the two events that belong forever to the way of the Son: his cross and resurrection.

CHAPTER 4

The Cross: Love as Unconditional

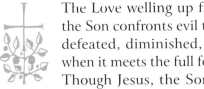The Love welling up from the Father and expressed in the Son confronts evil through the cross. But Love is not defeated, diminished, or changed into something else when it meets the full force of evil. Love is unconditional. Though Jesus, the Son of the Father, is rejected, condemned, and executed, the Love that he embodied kept on being Love "to the end" (John 13:1b). Far from being changed into hatred or resentment, God's love outstrips all human limits and contradictions. In this, it outwits the wisdom of a world built on revenge and retaliation. The light of Love is not overcome by the darkness of evil (John 1:5). By suffering the cross, Love shines in its true radiance even at that dark point and so exposes the power of evil for what it is. The excess of evil is met with the greater excess of Love.

In the mystery of the cross, Love claims even the dreaded realm of death to display its generosity. Love absorbs the menace of death into itself. As a result, death no longer appears as a fearful barrier cutting us off from life and from the God of life and love. Death now is revealed as the extreme to which God's love has gone, and the cross becomes the revelation of divine compassion and mercy. By being exposed to the power of evil and by not being overcome by it, the "Lamb of God . . . takes away the sin of the world" (John 1:29). The Lamb who was slain (Rev 5:7) has become the "atoning sacrifice for our sins . . . [and] also for the sins of the whole world" (1 John 2:2).

Though Christ's love unto death for "his own who were in the world" (John 13:1), history's vicious circle of lovelessness has been arrested. It is replaced by a new movement, that of an opening circle of love and reconciliation: "But if anyone does sin, we have an advocate with the Father, Jesus Christ the righteous" (1 John 2:1b). Faith is familiar with the conflict between an ever-vulnerable love and the violence of human selfishness. The disciples of Jesus are summoned into a life of genuine loving: "We know love by this, that he laid down his life for us—and we ought lay down our lives for one another" (1 John 3:16). Love is to be lived out not as a sweet emotion but in the sober realism of sacrificing ourselves in the service of others. The demands of love are always excessive. But our loving, however hesitant or defective, lives from the prodigality of the Love that goes beyond all human limits: "We will reassure our hearts before him whenever our hearts condemn us; for God is greater than our hearts" (1 John 3:19-20).

Thus, the Love that has been revealed remains true to itself, even at the darkest point of rejection. As Paul would say, it appears as the "weakness of God." Love refuses to be anything but itself even when confronted with violent rejection. A divine "folly" has worked to undermine the self-centered calculations of human wisdom (1 Cor 1:25).

II

The Gospel speaks of Jesus as the only Son from the Father (cf. John 1:14). But it is the will of the Father that this Son be not spared suffering, death, and the most gruesome form of execution. Yet Love would be contradicted if the Father demanded this death as a human sacrifice to appease his anger. Such a sense of God is suggested in the biblical story of Abraham called to sacrifice his son, Isaac. This violent manifestation of primitive religion continues to shock.[1] In the world of Christian faith, however, it is God the Father who gives up his beloved Son. The cross, then, is Love's self-sacrifice. In order to reverse the cycles of revenge and violence that bedevil human history, "God so loved the world that he gave his only Son" (John 3:16).

Jesus' unique relationship to the God whom he invoked as "Abba, Father" promised no escape from the fate of witnessing to Love in a loveless world. In the cause of that Love, Jesus contested the violence of his world and the history that shaped it. The cross of his sufferings was not the result of trying to manipulate reality in accord with some infantile fantasy or adult delusion. It was the predictable outcome of Jesus' unflinching affirmation of reality. The truth of that reality ran counter to the violence inherent in any kind of diseased justice that sought to enlist religion to bolster an inhuman situation. The Father, in whose name Jesus acted, was the God who would reign in a kingdom "not from this world" (John 18:36). In that kingdom of God, all the self-serving projects of worldly glory come to naught (see John 8:54). Because of his dedication to the kingdom of God, the Son met his death. But this would mean that the realm of God would now be open and welcoming to the hopeless, the poor, and the diseased—in a word, to all for whom routine religion offered no hope. Those who followed the way of Jesus had to "be merciful, just as your Father is merciful" (Luke 6:36), while praying with realism, "Father, . . . forgive us our sins, for we ourselves forgive everyone indebted to us" (Luke 11:2, 4).

The kind of love that is here revealed leaves no room for sentimental self-indulgence. It inspires the freedom of personal responsibility and compassion for the suffering other. Given over to the will of the Father, Jesus involves himself with sinners and outcasts. He contests the false gods of his time and ours, and he rejects the violence and oppression they sanction. The world reacted, and there was, then, a price to be paid in the currency of condemnation, execution, and worldly failure. The Beloved Son enjoyed no privileged position (Heb 5:7-9). He did not ask for "more than twelve legions of angels" (Matt 26:53) to come to his aid; nor did the Father send them. God has given what is most intimately his own into the alien, self-enclosed reality of the world in order to break open to life in its fullness.

III.

God as acted "for us" and "for our sake," as the Creed has it. These phrases are not expressions of abstract and general religious information, but rather the language of Love. They indicate God's free self-commitment to each and to all. The gift of God can never be fully described. The Son is incarnate as truly human and exposed to all human limitations. He knows the darkest of all human experiences—failure, betrayal, condemnation, torture, execution, burial as a criminal.

Yet to be "for us" is the basic impetus of Jesus' life and mission. He lives to do God's loving will and acts as "the good shepherd" who lays down his life for his flock (cf. John 10:15-17). His divine character as Son of the Father makes him uniquely related to all. His whole being is offered to nourish us, for whose sake he lived and died. Addressing the disciples in a final meal, he said, " 'Take, eat; this is my body.' Then he took a cup, and after giving thanks he gave it to them, saying, 'Drink from it, all of you; for this is my blood of the covenant, which is poured out for the many for the forgiveness of sins' " (Matt 26:26-28).

Though John's Gospel does not contain a Eucharistic formula of institution like the other gospels, it does lead its readers into a deep understanding of the Eucharist, especially in chapter 13. Jesus is focused on a decisive moment: when "Jesus knew that his hour had come" (John 13:1). It is *his* hour, the climax toward which the Father's will had guided him. It is also his hour because it is his Father's hour. In it the whole course of human history will be condensed and fulfilled, for Jesus is about to "depart from this world and go to the Father" (John 13:1). In life, and now in the death he is about to die, Jesus has been moving toward the Father. Jesus has passed through a world of conflict, division, rejection, and terminal antagonism toward the true God. Throughout his mission, he has been intent on opening that world to the loving presence of the Father. In his return to the Father, God will be revealed to the world as its original lover and the source of deathless life (John 3:16).

The more Jesus moves toward the Father, the more he manifests the Love that God is: "Having loved his own who were in the world, he loved them to the end" (John 13:1). In going to the God who so loved the world, the Son embodies the limitless extent of the Father's love. His love is tested against the power of evil: "The devil had already made up his mind that Judas Iscariot . . . would betray him" (John 13:2).[2] Love is at work not only in the teeth of diabolic machinations but even in this disciple's betrayal. Love keeps on being Love even at such extremes.

By washing his disciples' feet, the Son reveals the true character of the Father. His gesture sums up all his words and deeds to this point and anticipates the full meaning of the hour that has now arrived. God's glory is a scandal to all worldly pretensions. The Son's inglorious departure from this world through condemnation and crucifixion will reveal glory of another kind.

What we have here expressed is the movement of truly personal life—both in the case of God and of humanity made in God's image. In the deepest sense of the word, personal existence is with and for others. In being for us, Jesus is the living revelation among us of the divine life to which we are called. Not only does he reveal such a form of life as a model and a promise, he nourishes his followers into it, as they eat and drink the reality of his Body and Blood and breathe his Spirit. The logic of Christian life is inescapable: "Just as I have loved you, you also should love one another" (John 13:34). Such is the meaning of the Eucharist, a sharing in the self-giving love of Christ.

For his part, Paul chides the Philippians to "look not to your own interests, but to the interests of others" (Phil 2:4). He invites them to imitate the self-giving character of Jesus: "Let the same mind be in you that was in Christ Jesus" (v. 5). The truth of Jesus' divine identity was manifested in his unreserved service of others: "though he was in the form of God, . . . [he] emptied himself, taking the form of a slave" (Phil 2:6-8). In an intensely personal moment, Paul can claim that his whole life is sustained by his relation to "the Son of God who loved me and gave himself for me" (Gal 2:20).

IV

The parables that came from the lips of Jesus turned the ordinary world upside down. His way of imagining what mattered was different. He called into question entrenched systems of worldly power and status. His aim was to summon the world out of its desperately self-destructive ways and into a universe of grace and mercy. So radical was his voice that the cross awaited him.

Execution by crucifixion was employed by the Roman authorities precisely because of its obscene impact. It was a mode of execution reserved for slaves and subverters of the empire, a gruesome deterrent against those who were deemed to be "nonpersons" because of their threat to society. It was only after crucifixion as a form of execution had been abolished by Emperor Constantine in the fourth century that the cross became a Christian symbol. It is difficult for anyone today to capture the sense of emotional and cultural shock that resulted from connecting God, Christ, or divine Love to such a hideous form of death. To affirm that the true God was revealed in such a way meant both scandal to religious people and utter foolishness to the philosophers. The real God, the creator of all things, could not act like *that*! In Paul's language in 1 Corinthians 1:20-25, Jesus crucified is a stumbling block to those of his own people who looked for a more obviously triumphant messiah. The Gentile philosophers conceived of a divine reality utterly unaffected by evil and suffering. That supreme reality had to be incapable of suffering, immutable, inhuman, and ultimately unconcerned. For them, the cross was a folly of the most fundamental kind. And, of course, any linking of this criminal executed by Roman authority to the revelation of the one true God had to be profoundly subversive of the fabric of the imperial power. The quasi-divine, imperial Caesar bore no resemblance to this condemned and executed criminal. Yet Paul defiantly insisted that the "foolishness of God," acting in this shameful death, was the source of all wisdom: "For God's foolishness is wiser than human wisdom, and God's weakness is stronger than human strength" (1 Cor 1:25).

While there is nothing morbid or voyeuristic as the early Christians "proclaim[ed] the Lord's death until he comes" (1 Cor 11:26), there is an unflinching realism in their accounts of what took place. The Gospel of Mark depicts the agony of Jesus as intense isolation. He is offered the cup of complete earthly failure. The world bears down on him as utterly opaque to the light of God. There is no sign of the Father's presence. Mark's Gospel speaks of him beginning to be "distressed and agitated" and of how he felt a deep grief "even to death" (Mark 14:33). He falls to the ground, praying that the hour might pass. So much does he feel the infinite weight of the world's fate that Luke adds the graphic detail of the bloody sweat (Luke 22:44).

In this state of utter collapse, with his disciples asleep and the triumph of his enemies impending, he is stripped of everything except his character as Son. Nothing else remains. Even the disciples flee. This terminal moment wrings from him an act of unreserved surrender to the One from whom he came: "Abba, Father, for you all things are possible; remove this cup from me; yet, not what I want, but what you want" (Mark 14:36). The Father is the God of Love's limitless possibilities. In the Son's compassionate solidarity with all who resist evil and struggle in the cause of good, everyone is embraced by a love and mercy beyond anything the human mind can imagine. The kingdom will come on its own terms and in its own time, and Love must conquer on its own terms: "Put your sword back into its place; for all who take the sword will perish by the sword" (Matt 26:52).

The gospels recall a sorry cycle of betrayal and desertion. One of Jesus' disciples, Judas, betrays him to the parties plotting for months to destroy him. They hand him over to the Jewish leaders. From the Sanhedrin he is taken to the Roman governor. Pilate passes him along to the local puppet king. Herod sends him back to Pilate. The governor offers him to the mercy of the mob. And so, betrayed by one of his own, denied by the leader of those he had chosen to walk with him, left for lost by the rest of them, despised now by his own people, libeled by false witnesses, he is condemned in the courts of the secular and religious authorities of his time. Then, after being tortured by the police and soldiers guarding him, he is taken to be executed in the hideous manner of crucifixion.

Throughout the whole drama of Jesus' condemnation and execution, it is as though the powers of evil are defying God to reveal himself. God would not be God if the kingdom that Jesus proclaimed ended in futility. And it would be worse than failure if the Father's intention to save and forgive was changed into vengeance and became some worldly display of power. To answer evil with evil, as though the law of "an eye for an eye and a tooth for a tooth" guided God's own behavior, would be the flat contradiction of all that Jesus stood for. But there is no divine vengeance. Love does not turn to hatred and revenge. God is no self-serving worldly power, and the Father sends no legion of angels. For the God of Jesus has refused to have any presence in the world save that of the crucified Son. And, as this Son prays for the forgiveness of those who have crucified him, he rejects any worldly identity, any worldly justification or protection, save what Love can reveal.

The cross scoops out of mind, heart, and imagination all diseased and distorted notions of God. By killing Jesus, the power of evil challenges the mystery of God to reveal itself for what it is. And precisely when human sensibilities were so shocked, the utter excess of divine Love was displayed. In the cross of Jesus, the excess of evil was met with that excess of Love which nothing in all creation could gainsay. In the providence of Love working through all events, the most obscene gesture of human evil became the occasion for the disclosure of the prodigality of God's love for sinful humanity: "Christ died for the ungodly. . . . God proves his love for us in that while we were yet sinners Christ died for us" (Rom 5:6, 8). That "for us" of Christ's self-giving goes to an unimaginable limit. It finds us at that point where our history is found to be most against God and most enclosed within the desperate circle of violence and lovelessness.

The cross was a seismic culture shock for the religious and philosophical sensibilities of the day. Christians proclaimed that there was another kind of power at work, an infinite compassion acting only in the vulnerability and evidence of Love. Paul could write, "God's foolishness is wiser than human wisdom, and God's weakness is stronger than human strength" (1 Cor 1:25). Every religious hope, every philosophical system, every political power had to be jolted by such a brutally countercultural event: "For the message of the cross is foolishness to those who are perishing, but to us who are being saved it is the power of God" (1 Cor 1:18).

The crucifixion of Jesus was not the result of the imposition of some capricious divine test or punishment. For Jesus, it was the fate entailed in his refusal to be anything but exclusively for the Father and totally dedicated to his reign. For his part, the Father, "the Almighty," refuses any other presence in the world except that of his crucified Son. The Spirit will act in no other way, will show no other power, except that self-giving love whereby the Father gives his Son and the Son surrenders all to the Father for our sake. Jesus was not the victim of a blind fate or a capricious divine will. God, in sending his Son, was not intent on entering the world as a superpower, taking revenge and putting down all opposition. The God whom Jesus represented was otherwise. Who *this* God was, what serving *this* God meant, how *this* God valued human beings—especially those considered worthless in any social and cultural system—were questions to be answered only within the reign of God that Jesus proclaimed.

The Son was truly human and the Word was truly made flesh, to the point of suffering a shameful death. He was swallowed up into the silence and darkness that mark every death. And in his death there were further agonies of mind and body as he suffered betrayal, abandonment, condemnation, torture, mockery, failure, execution. He suffered death as one put to death in what seemed an utterly God-forsaken world. His vulnerability came from his being totally for God in a world where God did not seem to figure. There, the "reign of God" seemed completely powerless, and love, if it meant anything, was best kept for one's own. In molding that world, other forces were far more successful than love ever could be. To this degree, Jesus died *of* God, because he had been so much *from* God and *for* God. He breathed his last in surrender to his Father's will—and he hung before the world as a crucified corpse. He loved his own unto the end.

With the burial of that tortured body, the God of love was, to all intents and purposes, also buried. Jesus and his God are buried in a black hole in which all that Love promises is swallowed up and comes to nothing. He goes down into the world of the dead. As the Apostles' Creed so enigmatically puts it, "he descended into hell." However we imagine this state, he goes down to the point we most dread, where death is at its deadliest and no hope is left. Through Jesus' death and burial, Love claims as its own the most dreadful dimensions of human experience. It embraces the whole of human grief over the ending of all communication with others. Love thus enters into that region of the lost when the proclaimer of the kingdom of God now lies dead in a stranger's tomb. Love knows the world of the dead. The Son is "for us" not only on the surface of life but also in the depths, within the whole lost past of our world.

And so, through this longest of days, faith must wait in emptiness and grief for Love to reveal itself, until Christians can call that day Holy Saturday.

The Scriptures represent in various ways the emergence of a new community gathered around the crucified Christ: Simon of Cyrene, the courageous presence of the faithful women, the "Good Thief" making his last prayer, Mary and the Beloved Disciple at the foot of the cross, the Roman centurion declaring Jesus to be innocent, and Joseph of Arimathea asking Pilate for the body. By dying on the cross, the man of parables becomes the supreme parable designed to express how God can undo the evil of the world and form our humanity anew.

The solemn reading in the liturgy of Good Friday is introduced as "The Passion of Our Lord Jesus Christ according to John." It tells a too familiar story, until we appreciate it as the love story of God's immersion in our world. It tells of a terrible cost in terms of pain, sorrow, failure, and forgiveness. Any great love costs a life: "Having loved his own who were in the world, he loved them to the end" (John 13:1) despite betrayal and denial on the part of his disciples, despite the mockery and rejection of others, and despite condemnation, torture, and execution inflicted by those who ruled his world. It was a story of appalling tragedy, yet, as recorded in this gospel, not without hints of majesty. We are drawn into a center of tranquillity in the storm of suffering, where the Love not of this world knew what it was about, beyond anything that world could imagine.

There are as many ways of hearing this story as there are people and different ages of human history. Countless generations have listened and found in their different ways that here is the whole and healing truth. The Good Friday liturgy allows us simply to behold Jesus, and look even at each other, with a heart disarmed. It brings home to us that the way of the church is always a movement toward the cross where the passion of God is on display. It invites us to feel the depths of suffering that so often hide deeper than any words can express—in each of our lives, in the church itself, in the world at large.

As we pray in the liturgy on Good Friday, "Behold the wood of the Cross / on which hung the salvation of the world." The cross is unveiled in order to touch our hearts, as the faithful are invited to venerate it with a kiss, a touch, a genuflection, or a bow. The eyes of faith see the cross against the horizon of all our questions, fears, and hopes. By contemplating the wounded body hanging there, we are in the presence of the fathomless Love that has reached out into creation to find each one in this moment. In whatever the darkness, a light has begun to shine. Faith is not peering into a void marked only by a cross but is meeting the gaze of the Love that has been revealed. It has kept on being Love, and it has never been changed into something else—never less that itself and ever more than the heart dares to imagine. The cross shows Love exposed to death, not as its defeat but as the limit to which such love has gone.

The eyes of faith see the Father through the image of the crucified Son as the original Love that inexhaustibly gives itself—despite the ruthless hardness of the world. Love keeps on being Love, displayed as an ever more tender compassion and unreserved mercy.

As the cross points up to God, its arms point out to the world. We see embodied in the crucified Jesus the whole agony and pain of our world. Enfleshed in him are all the sufferings of the innocent, even the more dreadful sufferings of the guilty, for he bore our sins. He too dwells in the shadow of death and goes through the bitter valley of suffering.

All our human solutions seem useless if we dare to make eye contact with even one of the uncounted millions who have gone down in defeat. We think of our dear ones whose lives seem to have met up with unbearable tragedy. Beyond them, in the grim regions of suffering and isolation, there are the nameless crowds of the slave camps, of the mass graves, and of the starving children, the poor, and the tortured—the detritus of history.

Yet here too the cross is grace for us. It jolts us out of ourselves into the immense family of human suffering. It demands that we bear one another's burdens, and it serves as a signpost for the path along which we fear to travel—toward those places and people where hope has no voice unless it is ours:

> For I was hungry and you gave me food, I was thirsty and you gave me something to drink, I was a stranger and you welcomed me, I was naked and you gave me clothing, I was sick and you took care of me, I was in prison and you visited me. (Matt 25:34-36)

Again from the liturgy of Good Friday, we pray, "We adore you, O Christ, and we praise you, because by your holy cross, you have redeemed the world." The cross is anchored in the hard rock of the world. Unless this One had gone before us and known the regions we most fear, we are left alone with our lost selves. Love speaks when the crucified One whispers his word of hope, "Come to me, all you that are weary and are carrying heavy burdens, and I will give you rest" (Matt 11:28).

CHAPTER 5

The Resurrection:
Love as Transformative

 God is Love in its power to transform—first, with regard to Jesus himself, and then, for those who follow him. Love has not been defeated by evil and death. The resurrection occurs as a world-transforming event. In Christ's rising from the tomb, the Love that God is, that gave what is most intimately its own into the deepest darkness of the world, is finally revealed as victorious. Already the decisive transformation has occurred. As the energy stronger than any death we know, Love has had its way.

The liturgy abounds in marvelous hymns. Each Easter we hear the *Exsultet* sung in praise of the paschal candle, symbol of the Light of the World. The words seem to have an afterlife of resonance in the heart, which is a good indicator of great poetry:

> Exult, let them exult, the hosts of heaven,
> exult, let Angel ministers of God exult,
> let the trumpet of salvation
> sound aloud our mighty King's triumph!
> Be glad, let earth be glad, as glory floods her,
> ablaze with light from her eternal King,
> let all corners of the earth be glad,
> knowing an end to gloom and darkness.

This great Easter hymn acclaims "the sanctifying power of this night" and ends with this prayer:

> May this flame be found still burning
> by the Morning Star:
> the one Morning Star who never sets,
> Christ your Son,
> who, coming back from death's domain,
> has shed his peaceful life on humanity,
> and lives and reigns for ever and ever.

When the New Testament speaks of the resurrection, it does so only from within the reality itself. It is not so much talking *about* an event in a dispassionate, objective manner, but passionately participating *in* it and living *from* it. The gospels aim to bring their readers into a relationship with the crucified and risen Lord.

There are four implications in the meaning of the resurrection. First of all, it means that Christ Jesus is now present to the community of faith in the totality of what and who he is. In proclaiming the reign of God, he had indeed preached and taught and healed and acted. He had lived for the cause of his Father; and by suffering rejection, betrayal, and condemnation, he had died for it. But now, with his resurrection, he is given back to the faithful in the fullness of his reality. He is disclosed in his identity of being uniquely and wonderfully from God, of God, in all that he was, is, and will be. As Son of the Father, the risen One is able to be for us and with us, beyond the limitations of time and space. He is present in the love, power, and vitality of God. In this deep sense, the resurrection confirms the identity and mission of Jesus as the savior of the world.

Furthermore, in his rising from the dead and in his presence to believers, Jesus has not ceased to be the Word Incarnate. Rather, the incarnation is an ever-expanding event, opening out to new dimensions through Christ's resurrection and ascension. In Jesus' triumph over death, the reign of God is irreversible. God is with us in a new way, and our humanity already begins to live in a God-given fullness. By rising from the tomb, Jesus returns in the power of God in a manner that is beyond the reach of death, despair, and limited expectations. He comes as the One who has received the Father's affirmation and who is now accessible to all, beyond the limitations of time and space, through the Holy Spirit.

Second, in the resurrection Jesus is given back to his disciples as sheer gift. He becomes victoriously present in all that he is—in his words and deeds, in his body and spirit, in his identity and mission. He is now, in person, pure grace, blessing, and healing, given back to the world that had rejected him. Such a gift and such a form of giving surpass every imaginable kind of giving and restoration. Jesus is not simply resuscitated, for he has died to this life. He is not a ghost or a pure spirit; he is present in a new and wonderful form of life, yet in a palpable, bodily reality.

Nor was the resurrection of the crucified Jesus a particular instance of a more general expectation. After all, in the time of Jesus, the Sadducees did not believe in the resurrection, and the Pharisees associated such a hope only with the saints on the last day. Moreover, the prevailing currents of Greek philosophy would have found any suggestion of a new embodied existence far too materialistic. Besides, the expectations of the disciples themselves had collapsed in disillusionment. Against such an unpromising background, the raising up of the Crucified is God's great surprise. It comes from outside the scope of the theologies, the philosophies, and even the prayers of the world he lived in.

Third, if the resurrection is God's surprise, it is this most of all when it is considered as the outpouring of limitless mercy. The risen Jesus personifies sheer forgiveness. Love has not turned into rejection or vendetta. It has kept on being itself, to prove not only stronger than death but also more powerful than the weight of shameful evils that had worked to destroy Christ and negate his mission. He is risen not to reproach the disciples with their failures but to draw them beyond their previous doubts into his eternal life and to be his witnesses to the world. John's Gospel describes the merciful grace of the risen Christ as he breathes forth the Spirit on the disciples:

> Jesus said to them again, "Peace be with you. As the Father has sent me, so I send you." When he had said this, he breathed on them and said to them, "Receive the Holy Spirit." (John 20:21-23)

The merciful presence of the risen One changes the disciples: once forgiven themselves, they are sent forth as the agents of divine forgiveness.

Fourth, the resurrection of Jesus inspires the mission of the church. Energized by the resurrection, faith, far from being distracted into some otherworldly realm, is impelled to witness to how the world has been changed in its depths by what happened in this transforming event. An expanding circle of community unfolds from the risen One in order to include all peoples of all times and places and to embrace even the whole of creation. The disciples are sent into the world, now aware of belonging to a new humanity as it has been realized in Christ. Relationships based on division and mutual recrimination are abolished in the open circle of Love radiating out from what has happened in the resurrection of Christ. The ancient antagonism existing between Israel as "God's chosen people" and the "the nations" of the world is healed at its root:

> For he is our peace; in his flesh he has made both groups into one and has broken down the dividing wall, that is, the hostility between us. . . . So he came and proclaimed peace to those who were far off and peace to those who were near; for through him both of us have access in one Spirit to the Father. (Eph 3:14, 17-18)

In short, Jesus has returned to his own as "the resurrection and the life" (John 11:25). He comes to give his peace and to share the joy of his victory over the powers of evil. He introduces his disciples into the communion of life and love that he, the Son, enjoys with the Father. Transformed himself, he transforms others. He is in person the "word of life," the "life [that] was revealed," the "eternal life that was with the Father and was revealed to us" (1 John 1:1-2). God is Love as the life force that rolled back the tombstone of all human defeat and raised Jesus from the dead. Already, Love plants the seed of eternal life in all believers. God is proved to be the God of life and of the love that makes all things new.

II

Indeed, the resurrection of the Crucified is the event that most affects human history. It shocks time into another shape. Before Jesus was raised from the tomb, what people most valued was always at the mercy of what they most feared. The dreadful power of evil and the lethal finality of death held sway over the long, ambiguous passage of time. History ran on, forever inconclusive and undecided. Eras of progress or decline came and went. There was no decisive point. Some might have revered Jesus of Nazareth as one of the many good people who, despite a noble vision, were eventually found out by the harsh reality of the real world. For them, his "resurrection," if it meant anything, would be just a poetic way of saying that goodness will out in the long run. That might have been a consoling thought even if history remained a catalog of horrors and defeats. The dead stay dead, and any suggestion of someone rising from the dead had to be an embarrassment, even in religious circles.

For Christians, however, Christ's rising from that tomb of disgrace, defeat, and execution is the event that makes all the difference. He embodied a love stronger than death and dying. In that light of the resurrection, the terrible Friday of condemnation, torture, defeat, and execution is now known as the *Good* Friday. It is the astonishing revelation of an all-merciful love embracing the world at the level of its deepest darkness. From then on, the shocking scandal of the death of Jesus on the cross is understood as the revelation of the transforming power of God's love.

If there were no resurrection, thought Paul, then the love of the Father would be defeated, God would be misrepresented, Christian preaching would be in vain, faith would be futile, and hope would be an illusion—and "you are still in your sins" (1 Cor 15:17). But because the love of God has overcome all the evils that had been intensely concentrated in the cross, the resurrection of Jesus is the focus of Christian hope: "But in fact Christ has been raised from the dead, the first fruits of those who have died. . . . For as all die in Adam, so all will be made alive in Christ" (1 Cor 15:20, 22). A divinely wrought transformation has taken place in human history. It anticipates the ultimate triumph of God's saving plan: "When all things are subjected to him, then the Son himself will be subjected to him who put all things in subjection under him, so that God may be all in all" (1 Cor 15:28).

Faith in the resurrection does not only mean that something momentous happened in the past. From this uniquely saving event arose a new comprehension of everything in the past and in the future. The disciples now recalled what had been happening before they understood what was going on. Now they understood, and they looked forward to what would keep on happening. They now possessed a new sense of how God is present and acting both in history and in the universe itself.

The resurrection is a culminating event in the history of God's self-revelation. It throws light on the whole reality of how, what, and who God can be "for us men and for our salvation." In that luminous awareness, the gospels were written. They are not simple records of what Jesus said and did and suffered. Nor are they merely interpretations imposed on what had happened. In the radiance of what did happen—that event that had been missing in the world up to that point—the gospels communicate the whole saving truth of what had taken place. The early witnesses were so secure in their new knowledge that they were freed to admit the ignorance and puzzlement they had previously experienced. They could recall Jesus' teaching and questions, his riddles, parables, and hints—and their own resistance, confusion, and false expectations. They had noted with alarm his predictions of impending crisis, even while witnessing the wonder of his miracles and acts of forgiveness. They had felt the sheer authority of his presence and had heard his promise of a new age of unlimited grace. But they had expected something quite different. Now, however, they saw what it all had meant and what was going on all the time. They now had the key, and that key was an event so momentous that all their humbling remembrance of the past had to be reshaped if they were going to tell the world what had happened and what it all meant. And so the New Testament documents—inspired writings for the life of faith—were composed with an extraordinary creativity. The writers involved had to find words where no words were easily found. They had to re-read the precious writings of the past from a vantage point never accessible before. Faith in the risen Jesus meant that the whole world as they had known it had been made new.

Jesus told many parables in his preaching. They made his hearers see their ordinary world upside down—how things looked in the sight of God. But behind all the parables of Jesus was the supreme parable of his life, death, and resurrection. In him, the world has been made new, and life is filled with unimaginable promise. Life without end has begun; the world is being renewed in its youth.

The traditional expression of the Creed "on the third day" marks a historical memory of three decisive days. That Friday ended in the shock and grief of Jesus' execution, while Saturday dawned as a dreadful day of emptiness. Then, on Sunday, something happened as indescribable then as it is now. In the light of this eventful Sunday, that Friday of grief and shame would be called "Good," and the silence and darkness of that Saturday would be called "Holy."

The reference to the three days also locates the testimony of various witnesses of what took place. These men and women—Mary Magdalene, the other women, Peter, and the other disciples—could each recall a defining moment when their sorrow turned to joy. Their world could never be the same again. The phrase "on the third day" in its biblical meaning suggests a sense of something happening in God's good time. It looks to the moment when God will act to reveal his glory and saving power; as we read in Exodus, "Prepare for the third day, because on the third day the LORD will come down upon Mount Sinai in the sight of all the people" (Exod 19:11), and then, "On the morning of the third day there was thunder and lightning, as well as a thick cloud on the mountain. . . . Moses brought the people out of the camp to meet God" (Exod 19:16-17). The implication is that God has time for his people even when it seems that time has run out for them. The "third day" of God's intervention dawns beyond the "tomorrow" of human calculation or prediction. God acts in God's own time. It gives time for faith to experience the depths of human need and to awaken in longing for what only God can do. As the prophet Hosea proclaims, "After two days he will revive us; on the third day he will raise us up, that we may live before him" (Hos 6:2).

And so the three holy days: the Friday of the dying when Love goes "unto the end"; the Saturday of waiting for what only such Love can do; and then the Sunday where Love is revealed in its transforming power.

III

The novelty and surprise of the resurrection is necessarily related to the reality of the empty tomb. Its discovery is fixed "on the third day," just as it contains a personal reference to "some women of our group" (Luke 24:22) who reported it. On the one hand, it never was, and could never be, that Christian faith could find its energy by focusing on the mere emptiness of the tomb. Indeed, in the original accounts such emptiness gave rise only to further perplexity and fear (cf. Mark 16:8; Luke 24:5:11). The angels at the tomb made quite clear that there was no point in seeking the living among the dead (Luke 24:57). The joy of the disciples arose not from peering into an empty tomb but from their encounter with the crucified Lord coming to them as now alive and life-giving. These early witnesses had no inclination to haunt a grave site. They did not linger among the dead. Life now consisted in a full-bodied connection with the risen Jesus. This Jesus who had been crucified was now the form and the source of a new and ultimate vitality. In fact, the disciples' assurance of Jesus' victory over death stands in clear contrast to the original ambiguity they felt at finding his tomb empty.

Still, that emptiness did have its place in the full-bodied nature of their experience. Precisely as an index of the overbrimming reality of the resurrection, the blank fact of the empty tomb is lifted out of its original ambiguity. The inclusion of the empty tomb in the gospel accounts prevents faith from remaining on an idealist or mystical plane. To omit or downplay the testimony to the empty tomb is to find oneself veering very quickly into believing in a mere theology instead of the transforming divine happening that gives all theology a new reality to think about. Incidentally, to omit the evidence of the empty tomb means bypassing the special role of women in communicating the Gospel of new life! A legend would hardly base its case on the testimony of women in a culture that scarcely accepted their credibility.

This is to say that the empty tomb stands as a kind of historical marker for an overwhelming mystery. It expresses a demand— set right there in the history of human defeat and failure— for faith to be fully realistic. In a sense, the empty tomb is a negative sign: an absence pointing to a presence, an emptiness suggesting a new fullness, a darkness into which the light might shine. But faith in the resurrection is more. It is not satisfied, say, by merely putting a positive construction on the continuing significance of Jesus' message. The courage of Christian conviction is based on something more factual and objective. God has truly acted in raising up the Crucified in the reality of a world hitherto locked in death. In that assurance, faith comes to the tomb not to stay there but to break forth into a new sense of wonder. Because Christ is risen, everything is changed; the universe is now different. To enter into this empty tomb is to be challenged to stake all on the real victory of Love. The sting of death has been drawn (cf. Acts 2:31; 1 Cor 15:50-58).

The empty tomb plants the seeds of wonder and questioning in the ground of history. It is profoundly disturbing for any version of a world hermetically sealed against the extravagances of Love. For those grown suspicious of any good news, Jesus' rising from the tomb is simply too good to be true. Any life built on calculation and control does not usually welcome surprise.

There is no evidence of embarrassment over having to defend the emptiness of the tomb. Nor, for that matter, is there any indication that either friend or foe thought that the tomb contained the remains of Jesus. The gospel writer is quite aware of the allegation that the corpse had been stolen. That would have been a quite predictable explanation on the part of those for whom Jesus had to stay buried (see Matt 28:1-15)! Still, the fact that his corpse was not left moldering in a grave is never simply a proof of the resurrection. Believers must look elsewhere: "Why do you look for the living among the dead?" (Luke 24:5). Here, too, the emptiness of the tomb underscores the advantage of Jesus' going away (see John 16:7). Restricted by no earthly condition, held by no earthly tomb, he is present everywhere and to everyone as the source of ultimate life. To believe in him is to live in a universe that must allow for the impossible possibilities of God.

IV

The ascension of Christ points to the comprehensive sweep of God's love. Christ rises from the tomb and ascends into the luminous cloud of the divine presence. Jesus is no longer to be found in the time and space of his earthly life in Palestine. Nor is he accessible only through episodic appearances after his resurrection. He now fills all time and space. He inhabits every dimension of reality, from the highest realm of the infinite Godhead to the mundane, agonizing reality of created existence. The ascension opens the space in which believers of all times and nations can encounter Christ as the embodiment of the Father's love:

> But God, who is rich in mercy, out of the great love with which he loved us even when we were dead through our trespasses, made us alive together with Christ . . . and raised us up with him and seated us with him in the heavenly places. (Eph 2:4-6)

And so, the ascension of Jesus into heaven is not simply the end of the journey for him alone. It is of universal significance; a new beginning for all who will follow him, "so that in the ages to come [God] might show the immeasurable riches of his grace in kindness toward us in Christ Jesus" (Eph 2:7). The ascended Christ embodies the destiny to which all are called, "for we are what he has made us, created in Christ Jesus for good works, which God prepared beforehand to be our way of life" (Eph 2:10).

Though his passing from this world to the Father may be experienced as an absence, it is also a new presence in the sphere of faith: "And remember, I am with you always, to the end of the age" (Matt 28:20). Faith does not cling to Jesus as a localized cult object. By letting him go into the glory of the Father, believers receive him back in every moment and place and in the presence of the Spirit. The ascending Lord draws faith beyond the world of projections and fantasy. Consequently, to believe is not to look up into an imaginary heaven for a lost hero. The vision of faith sees Jesus as the One who has come, and will keep on coming, from out of the luminous reality of God into the reality of this world:

> As they were watching, he was lifted up, and a cloud took him out of their sight. While he was going and they were gazing up toward heaven, suddenly two men in white robes stood by them. They said, "Men of Galilee, why do you stand looking up toward heaven? This Jesus, who has been taken up from you into heaven, will come in the same way as you saw him go into heaven." (Acts 1:9-11)

By ascending, Jesus moves beyond the restrictions and limitations that structure our present human existence. The disciples as natives of Galilee must now live as citizens of a much larger world. The whole of creation is filled with Christ's saving presence. From the glory of heaven, the risen One fills the space left by his earthly absence. He has opened our earth to the hitherto hidden reality of heaven. Jesus had solemnly promised that the disciples "will see heaven opened and the angels of God ascending and descending upon the Son of Man"

(John 1:51). Jesus will be the new Jacob's ladder (Gen 28:12-17) connecting what is above with what is below. He will be in person the channel of a new communication between God and the world. In him we have the personal revelation of our Father in heaven: "Whoever has seen me has seen the Father. . . . Do you not believe that I am in the Father and the Father is in me?" (John 14:9-10).

The ascension does imply an ending. The privileged time of the eyewitness disciples who lived their lives at the historical beginnings of the Christian faith has come to an end. Now Christ is accessible only through their word and through the spiritual gift of faith: "Blessed are those who have not seen and yet have come to believe" (John 20:29). The new age has begun; the ascension of Jesus Christ now points into the space that God's love has made for the whole of human history to unfold in the freedom of faith.

The prayer of Jesus has been answered: "So now, Father, glorify me in your own presence with the glory that I had in your presence before the world existed" (John 17:5). In the answer to that prayer, all other prayers find their confidence and assurance. The Love that has made time for the universe of creation and for the free unfolding of human history has come to a glorious consummation. It is from that high point that further gifts are given: "Very truly, I tell you, if you ask anything of the Father in my name, he will give it to you. . . . Ask and you will receive, so that your joy may be complete" (John 16:23-24).

The ascension of the crucified and risen Jesus brings home the full scope of God's love for us. One of us, this man, Jesus of Nazareth, who had gone down into the dark pit of this world's sufferings, is now with the Father. Death has not slammed shut the door behind him. It stands forever ajar—in him who is with us and with God. His humanity has not been vaporized or annulled. Rather, he is the full-bodied actualization both of God's relationship to us and of our most intimate bonding with God. Because the Son remains forever human, because the Word does not shake off the flesh of his humanity, creation is transfigured. The universe, and we within it, has been drawn into the Love-life of the Trinity. Subsumed into Jesus' journey to the Father, the world has come to its final glory. While faith and hope must be patient with God's patience and have time for the whole of God's good time, the assurance remains: he is in that *there* which every *here* of our lives longs for.

Christ's return in glory will be the final act of God's self-manifestation. After Love has shown its patience with the dark ambiguities of our history and has had time for the full drama of human freedom, it will bring its own fulfillment. The groaning of all creation in travail, our own groaning as part of it, and the Spirit's groaning supporting our hopes (Rom 8) will end in the birth of the whole Christ. The truth will out. Love will remain. And Jesus Christ will be revealed as the "Yes" to all God's promises and as the "Amen" to all our prayers (see 2 Cor 1:20).

In Christ, risen from the tomb and ascended into heaven, God's judgment on the world takes place. Our responsibility as Christians is to pass no final judgment. To us is given the task of proclaiming his Gospel in patience and forgiveness, in giving and receiving, in dialogue among ourselves and with those who do not believe, and in holding the grace we have received as meant for all: "Do not judge, and you will not be judged. . . . Forgive, and you will be forgiven; give, and it will be given to you" (Luke 6:37-38). In deferring to God's judgment, believers must wait in a humble hope regarding their judgments of others. We cannot pass absolute judgment, for there is no kingdom of God on this earth, nor is there an empire of evil within history. In leaving final judgment to the God of love, we journey through time, waiting on a revelation of truth that can only occur at the end. As Paul writes,

> It is the Lord who judges me. Therefore do not pronounce judgment before the time, before the Lord comes, who will bring to light the things now hidden in darkness and will disclose the purposes of the heart. Then each one will receive commendation from God. (1 Cor 4:4-5)

And yet to believe in Christ as Judge is not to anticipate some new judgment to be passed on the world. That judgment has already been made. In the crucified and risen One, Love has not been turned into vengeance. It has kept on being Love, as expressed in Jesus' prayer for mercy: "Father, forgive them; for they do not know what they are doing" (Luke 23:34). The definitive character of the final judgment enacted in Christ is strongly expressed in John's Gospel:

> Indeed, God did not send the Son into the world to condemn the
> world, but in order that the world might be saved through him. . . .
> Those who do what is true come to the light, so that it may be
> clearly seen that their deeds have been done in God. (John 3:17, 21)

While we must allow for the possibility of created freedom to
reject Christ, it is still a universe of grace. God is not constrained by
unredeemed categories of worldly justice in which the penalty must
fit the crime. The saving character of divine judgment is already
revealed and enacted in Christ. Whatever the dreadful possibilities
of human freedom to reject the grace that is offered, the world, as
a whole, has been fundamentally saved. God's saving intention
will not be defeated: God *so* loved the world. However powerful
the resistance to grace might be in us or in others, we are never
entitled to lose hope in what God can do—and has already done.
An ultimate judgment has been made, and nothing in all creation
is able to thwart the impossible possibilities of God's love. While
the church celebrates the holiness of a many of its members, it has
never dared, for fear of denying the Gospel itself, to declare that
any human being is beyond the reach of divine mercy.

There are no ultimate judgments to be made in the course of
history—except that there is One who judges and that he loved us
until the end. Faith looks to a judgment beyond our history and
keeps its peace, content to leave all judgment to the Lord: "It is God
who justifies. Who is to condemn? It is Christ Jesus, who died, yes,
who was raised, who is at the right hand of God, who indeed inter-
cedes for us" (Rom 8:33-34). Whatever our burdens in this life, the
responsibility of making an ultimate judgment is not one of them.

The Creed's affirmation of a final divine judgment is, in effect,
an act of hope. Faith looks to a moment of truth when all that is
loveless and destructive in our experience of ourselves and of our
world will be revealed for what it is. God's love will come into its
own. What we most treasure is not indefinitely at the mercy of
what we most fear. Judgment, then, in its deepest Christian meaning is not an object of dread but an inspiration to eager desire and
prayer: "Marana tha!" (1 Cor 16:22);[1] "Amen. Come, Lord Jesus!"
(Rev 22:20). Fear, then, is not the best preparation for the judgment
that awaits us all, "the living and the dead":

God is love, and those who abide in love abide in God, and God abides in them. Love has been perfected among us in this: that we may have boldness on the day of judgment, because as he is, so are we in this world. There is no fear in love, but perfect love casts out fear; for fear has to do with punishment, and whoever fears has not reached perfection in love. We love because he first loved us. (1 John 4:16-19)

St. Thomas Aquinas writes of the power of the resurrection already causing our spiritual resurrection even though our full bodily sharing in the resurrection is still to come. Through the gift of sanctifying grace, we already share in the life of the Trinity, as children of the Father, members of Christ, and temples of the Spirit. Through the God-given virtues of faith, hope, and charity, as well as the further gifts of the Holy Spirit, Christian consciousness possesses a new wisdom and the energies of the love that never ends (cf. 1 Cor 13:8). All this brings a new taste to life and a new atmosphere. We can inhale the Spirit of creation transformed. The full transformation of all things in Christ is still ahead of us, but already the seeds of our new making have been sown. The harvest is already anticipated in the resurrection of the Crucified. Now that he is risen, life can never be the same again. The Love that God is has already acted and given a pledge of what is to come.

CHAPTER 6

The Holy Spirit:
Love as Communicative

 God is self-giving Love, ever active in every moment and in every life. The Father's original loving is from all eternity, even though it takes effect in time. But that is not to say that it is confined only to the distant past. Love pervades all times and directs the past, present, and future of our individual and collective existence. The Father's self-giving in the Son, the Son's love for his own "unto the end," his self-offering on the cross, and his victory in the resurrection are not events isolated in the past. Love is an endless outpouring. In the heart of God, the inexhaustible, overbrimming ecstasy and outreach of Love is the Holy Spirit.

I

The Spirit of truth and love is *the* gift of God. It enables us to receive the gifts of God in Christ. This Spirit is the divine witness to the victory of Christ for all believers throughout history. The Acts of the Apostles presents the promised Spirit coming to the disciples after the ascension as a baptism and power from on high to direct the church in its mission to the world (Acts 1:1-11; 2:1-47).

For Paul, the Spirit is more often presented as a divine field of energy—pouring forth the love of God in our hearts (Rom 5:5)—and as the promise of the resurrection for all who believe (Rom 8:11). This same Spirit forms the followers of Christ in a free, fearless relationship with the Father (Rom 8:14-17). The Holy Spirit is always working within us, both aiding human weakness and expanding Christian hopes "with sighs too deep for words" (Rom 8:26). Paul prays, "May the God of hope fill you with all joy and peace in believing, so that you may abound in hope by the power of the Holy Spirit" (Rom 15:13).

II

From the Johannine perspective, the Spirit comes from the Father—and from the risen and ascended Jesus—into the void left by Jesus' return to the Father. The "Spirit of truth" is sent into this space of absence as a permanent presence, witnessing to all that Jesus is. In this respect, the Spirit is intimately connected with the presence of the Son. John the Baptist had testified to the Spirit descending from heaven and remaining on Jesus to be the medium with which Jesus would baptize (John 1:32-33). Accordingly, in the experience of God's love, the Holy Spirit is a living stream emanating from the glorified Christ (John 7:37-39). John's Gospel portrays the gift of the Spirit as the last breath of the Crucified (John 19:30)—and the first breath of the risen One (John 20:22). In the ways of Love, the coming of the Spirit is the "advantage" that would follow the departure of Jesus from the earthly scene (John 16:7).

Emanating from Jesus, the Spirit always connects the Christian sense of God back to the life and death of the Son (John 16:14; 1 John 4:2-3; 2 John 1:7). The Spirit of truth guides those who follow the way of Christ into an ever-fuller realization of the form of true life (John 14:26). This gift of God in person is the Paraclete. He comes to strengthen believers in the midst of a world so enclosed in itself that it resists the prodigality of the Love that has been revealed. Despite their human weakness, believers will never lack *this* witness. The ever-greater testimony of the Spirit (1 John 5:9) will keep our consciousness of Love alive.

As a result, Christian experience is being conscious of living from a new center, the Love that God is. This kind of awakening is made possible "by the Spirit that [God] has given us" (1 John 3:24; cf. 4:13), for those who believe in Christ have "the testimony in their hearts" (1 John 5:10). As a result, those who have awakened to the love that God has for them abide in God, and God abides in them (1 John 4:13). In these different ways, the Holy Spirit is the Love that sustains and expands Christian experience throughout history.

The Creed confesses the Holy Spirit to be "the Lord, the giver of life." This divine presence moves within and among us in the power and energy of that abundant life promised by Jesus (John 10:10). As both divine Giver and divine Gift, the Spirit dwells in believers to open their lives to a new realm of relationships—to the Father, to Christ, and to one another. Where the Spirit is, there too are the Father and the Son; and where they are, there is an ever-open circle of love embracing all in a communion of life.

III

Through the gift of the Holy Spirit, Christ comes to us through a power not of this world. A properly divine creativity is at work before which the human mind and heart must stand silent. When this Spirit acts, "nothing will be impossible with God" (Luke 1:37). This "power at work within us is able to accomplish abundantly far more than all we can ask or imagine" (Eph 3:20). The scope of the Spirit's action, therefore, is not limited to any human measure or imagination. Breathed forth from the depths of God, the Spirit comes always as an excess, a surprise, and a gift. The prodigality of Love overbrims any finite anticipation or creaturely need on our part.

To adore the Spirit as the Third Person of the Trinity is to affirm the limitless originality of Love. Because the Spirit comes forth from the divine depths, the Spirit is like a great wave of life and love in which all becoming occurs. In the Spirit, the Word is eternally conceived, creation happens, the Word is made flesh, and the whole of creation moves toward its fulfillment. The Holy Spirit is breathed forth as Love for all that God is, for all that God can and will be, for all creation. The Spirit is Love unlimited, God's ecstatic self-giving outreach to all, both eternally and in time. The Father is, then, Love, self-expressive in the Word and self-giving in the Spirit. The Son is Love as the Word expressing all that God is. The Spirit is

Love welling up from the unity of the Father and Son to embrace all in a great community of life and love.

In every moment of creation, the Spirit, as the Lord and giver of life, has labored to bring forth life. This has culminated in the presence among us of Christ, "the resurrection and life" (John 11:25). The resurrection of Jesus reveals that God's Spirit of life is stronger than any death-dealing power. It animates the whole of groaning creation that it might bring forth the whole Christ in the full dimensions of "the life of the world to come." The One who brought about Love's victory in the life and death of Jesus is also at work within us:

> If the Spirit of him who raised Jesus from the dead dwells in you, he who raised Christ from the dead will give life to your mortal bodies also through his Spirit who dwells in you. (Rom 8:11)

The whole groaning reality breathes with this Holy Breath, as all lives move toward the fullness of life:

> For the creation waits with eager longing for the revealing of the children of God. . . . We know that the whole creation has been groaning in labor pains until now; and not only the creation, but we ourselves, who have the first fruits of the Spirit, groan inwardly while we wait for adoption, the redemption of our bodies. . . . Likewise the Spirit helps us in our weakness; for we do not know how to pray as we ought, but that very Spirit intercedes with sighs too deep for words. (Rom 8:19, 22-23, 26)

IV

The Spirit is at the heart of God's special, supremely personal mode of action. In the Bible's multifaceted witness, the Spirit is the cause of creation and life (Gen 1:2; Isa 32:15; 44:3-5; Ps 104:30). The Breath of God gave the heroes of Israel their liberating strength (Judg 3:10; 6:34; 11:29; 13:25; 14:6; 14:19; 1 Sam 10:6). The Spirit of wisdom enlightened the sages (Num 24:2; 2 Sam 23:2; Isa 9:5; 11:2) and inspired the prophets (Hos 9:7). The Spirit of God fills the world (Wis 1:7) and works in the successive generations of God's people to prepare it for what is promised (Gal 4:29). In the fullness of time, the power of the Spirit brings history to its peak, enabling Mary, the virgin daughter of Zion, to bring forth the Holy One. Jesus is conceived in the womb of his mother by the power of the Spirit who moves him, in turn, at every moment of his life and mission (Acts 10:38). Filled with the Spirit, Jesus performs his works of healing and liberation (Luke 4:14:18) and contends with the spirits of evil (Luke 11:20). As he surrenders his life to God for the sake of the kingdom, he offers himself "through the eternal Spirit" (Heb 9:14). And through the Spirit, the Father raises the crucified One from the dead (Rom 8:11), and the church is born (John 3:5; 7:37ff). As the radiance of the Spirit streams from the face of Christ, it transforms believers from glory to glory (2 Cor 3:18) to bring about a new Spirit-filled existence (1 Cor 15:44; Rom 8:11). If Jesus is the mediator between God and humanity, the Spirit is the medium in which God's transforming action takes place.

The traditional sequence—Father, Son, and Spirit—is followed by most theological expositions and by the Creed itself. This can have the unintended but still unfortunate result of reducing "the Third Divine Person" to very much an afterthought. But, in reality, the Spirit is the divine personal agent who first brings about the Son's incarnation in the world. Christian discourse, in its unending effort to express how God is Love, has never been constrained by an overly rigid ordering of the Divine Persons in a mathematical fashion as first, second, and third. It is one thing to use our human categories to express the meaning of the Trinity in some limited fashion; it is another thing to overlook the fact that the divine life of the Trinity is one eternal, infinite Act. Consequently, there is no language of "before" or "after" that is really appropriate when speaking of the life of God, since such categories belong to the created world of time. Even when we speak of the First, Second, and Third Divine Persons, that says more about our limited ways of understanding the eternal coming forth of the Word and Spirit within God. There is no question of imposing a temporal sequence on the eternal vitality of the Trinity.

Nonetheless, some knowledge is possible by way of analogy with our human experience. We are all conscious of knowing and loving. For instance, the more we know, the more we love the other; and the more we love, the deeper our knowledge of this other. That experience is of some value when we start reflecting on the divine consciousness. It is helpful to think of the Spirit as God's infinite power of loving. An ecstasy of love arises from the Father in the joy of knowing and uttering all that he is in the Word. The Spirit, given the limits of human imagination, both precedes and proceeds from the Son, for this Spirit is the divine power of Love in which the Father communicates himself in the Son. At the same eternal moment, in this Love the Son surrenders all to the Father. Hence, new ways of speaking can usefully be explored in order to counter the image of temporal sequence in which the Spirit always comes last. In fact, there is a less rigid pattern open to the play of the full range of biblical experience. For example, we read in Scripture that the Spirit brings forth, guides, anoints, and witnesses to Christ, the Word Incarnate. Then, too, we confess in the Creed itself that Jesus Christ "by the Holy Spirit was incarnate of the Virgin Mary, / and became man." In both cases, the implication is that the Father generates and directs the Son in the power of the Holy Spirit.

Christians adore the divine community of Father, Son and Spirit. God is not solitary, but is rather an unimaginable and unbounded Love-life of interpersonal giving and receiving. Worshipped and glorified with the Father and the Son, the Spirit is acknowledged as the living "space," as it were, of divine communion—the One in whom the Father and Son surrender to each other in mutual love and delight. For us human persons to receive the Spirit is to experience a divine impulse toward self-effacing service of the other. We register the presence of the Spirit in our midst in words of unity, love, peace, and generosity.

Our thoughts and prayers often celebrate how we belong "in the unity of the Holy Spirit." Nonetheless, we must always remember that the unity of the Spirit does not suppress personal distinctions—neither in God nor in the community of the church itself. It is therefore necessary to think of the presence of the Spirit as creating, preserving, and promoting among persons the reality of unity-in-distinction. Being a person is not to be cut off from others so as to be ever defending oneself against them. Rather, fully personal existence is to be "from and for the other" in loving interaction. In other words, to be a person, whether divine or human, is to be in relation. Indeed, a long tradition of theological language speaks of the reality of the three Divine Persons as pure relationships. In that understanding, the Father is pure "Sonwardness" in the Spirit, the Son is pure "Fatherwardness" in the same Spirit, and the Holy Spirit is pure "Father-and-Sonwardness." Admittedly, these are clumsy expressions, but they do point to the character of each of the Divine Persons as being from, for, and with the Others.

When the Creed, then, expresses adoration of the Spirit within the life of the Trinity, it is correcting any tendency to think of the Father and Son as locked in a self-enclosed kind of unity. There is always room for the Other, and it is in this Other that Love is fully expressed and unity achieved. It can be said that the Spirit is the divine space of allowing for and welcoming the other, opening all relationships to freedom, creativity, and self-surrendering love. As said above, the presence of the Spirit always allows for genuine otherness, both within God and in the world of creation.

While the worship of God the Trinity recognizes the infinite difference between the creator and the creature, such a perception arises out of a certain God-given "inside knowledge" of the divine life. The divine Three have drawn us, through the gifts of faith, hope, and love, into their own vitality. We adore the three Divine Persons and sing "Glory be to the Father and to the Son and to the Holy Spirit." There is, however, a more intimate formula: "Glory *to* the Father *through* the Son *in* the Holy Spirit." The believer does not behold God from the outside, as it were, but lives the divine life from within. To believe is to participate in the circulation of life and love that is the Trinity.

Our glorification of the Holy Spirit shares in the way the Father and the Son glorify the Spirit of their unity. As the Father glorifies the Son in the resurrection, the Son glorifies the Father by offering to him the whole of creation. But both Father and Son now glorify the Spirit: "When the Advocate comes, whom I will send you from the Father, the Spirit of truth who comes from the Father, he will testify on my behalf" (John 15:26). Jesus goes on to say, "It is to your advantage that I go away, for if I do not go away, the Advocate will not come to you" (John 16:7). Faith must make room for the originality of the coming of the Spirit: "When the Spirit of truth comes, he will guide you into all the truth" (John 16:13). It is the Father's will to be worshipped in "spirit and truth" (John 4:24). Both the Father and the Son are now present in the world in no way other than through this Holy Spirit. As they glorify their Spirit, the Spirit glorifies them. In this Spirit the Father is worshipped and the Son is glorified: "He will glorify me, because he will take what is mine and declare it to you" (John 16:14). As the Spirit dwells in believers, a life of self-surrendering love is present in the world.

Indeed, in the genesis of our faith in Christ and of our knowledge of the Father, the Holy Spirit is the first in the order of our experience. Only through the Spirit do we have any real contact with Christ and enter into an intimate relationship with the Father. There is more: through the Spirit, God brings the whole Christ into existence. From the act of creation to the formation of Israel and the faith of Mary, the Spirit is acting. From the incarnation of the Word to the resurrection of the Crucified, the power of the Spirit is at work. From the outpouring of Pentecost to the transformation of all creation and the life of the world to come, "the Lord, the giver of life" is unceasingly in action. All such mysteries are phases in the revelation of the Holy Spirit of God's love at work in creation. If the divine community is boundless self-giving Love, we most glorify God in receiving, living, and communicating that Love.

VI.

When Christian imagination is fixed on the Incarnation alone and neglects the gift of the Spirit, it tends to value above all a given ecclesiastical order—that is, the institutional shape of the church. As a result, the God-given Spirit is made to look like a divine afterglow once the channels of salvation are identified and the structures of authority are settled. The Spirit, in all the originality of the divine Gift, tends to be forgotten.

But faith remains alive by yielding to the Spirit of limitless creativity in giving and acting. The Spirit of God is never reducible to any created energy; it infinitely surpasses all the powers of the world. The Creator Spirit relativizes the power structures constituting the so-called real world of any given time. In being open to the Spirit's limitless possibilities and surprises, faith expands to its proper proportions. The glory of God's gift outstrips mere human potential. Our plans can never prescribe or predict how the Spirit will act. Paul reminds us that "we speak of things in words not taught by human wisdom but taught by the Spirit, interpreting spiritual things to those who are spiritual" (1 Cor 2:13).

In all this, the Holy Spirit is both a divine object of adoration and the One who inspires us to adore in the first place. Consequently, to believe in the Spirit is to adore Love communicating itself in our lives through the course of history. In the Spirit, Love keeps on being Love and brings all the good that God has done in Christ into this present moment.

The Love in which the Father and the Son are united is the divine *We*. Yet it reaches beyond itself to include the *we* of all believers in its embrace. As the last breath of the Crucified (John 19:30) and the first breath of the risen Lord (John 20:22), the Spirit is Christ's gift of the divine Love-life he has come to share.

In this way, trinitarian Love has enfolded us into its own life. It remains ever *beyond*, *before*, and *ahead of* us as Father. It is ever *with* us in the Son as the Word made flesh. And it is ever *within* and *between* us in the Spirit. The Holy Spirit dwells within us as the limitless outreach of Love and as the Breath and atmosphere of divine life. In this Spirit, the divine ecstasy enters into our existence as the energy of self-giving Love. In that ecstatic existence, the young see visions and the old dream dreams (Acts 2:17), and the church is invigorated with a variety of Spirit-given gifts (1 Cor 12:4-11): "To each is given the manifestation of the Spirit for the common good" (1 Cor 12:7).

Faith adores the Spirit of Love as Lord and God. The Spirit is no impersonal force but is a divine *You* within the Holy Trinity. As the shared "Breath" of Love within the divine life, the Spirit is given into the world of creation and brings together the followers of Christ in the community of the church—"in the unity of the Holy Spirit." Just as the Son is one in being with the Father, so the Spirit is one in being with the Father and the Son (Council of Constantinople, AD 381). The Holy Spirit comes from God not as a created energy, nor as a generalized creative force pervading creation, but as *God*. Like the Son, the Spirit is "God from God." Originating in the Father, the Spirit receives and communicates all that God is.

VII

Through the Spirit's inspiration, the energies of self-giving Love invigorate the ways in which we hope: "And hope does not disappoint us, because God's love has been poured into our hearts through the Holy Spirit that has been given to us" (Rom 5:5).

Further, the Spirit's vivifying presence offers intimacy and freedom with God. We are liberated to be "free and easy" with God and, like Jesus, to invoke the Father in the intimacy and familiarity connoted in the name Abba. In the Holy Spirit of this intimate sense of God, we can leave behind the idols fabricated by fearful human projections. When believers are possessed and illumined by the Spirit, they are enfolded into Christ's filial existence:

> For all who are led by the Spirit of God are children of God. For you did not receive a spirit of slavery to fall back into fear, but you have received a spirit of adoption. When we cry, "Abba! Father!" it is that very Spirit bearing witness with our spirit that we are children of God. (Rom 8:14-16)

Opposed to the Holy Spirit of truth and love is the world of unholy spirits. This is the world of obsessions and demonic drives that infest human life and culture. Such unholy spirits are destructive forces within society. The root of these self-destructive obsessions is the human capacity to deny the whole promise of life in order to make one's individual or social (or national) self the center of the universe to which all must bow. This distortion promises a spurious sense of power and control. Note that the word "diabolic" means, literally, "being torn apart" or being radically "distracted"—thus lacking any point of integration. When a person's individual or social existence is so torn and disintegrated, it is easy to fabricate idols. They are formed by projecting onto, say, possessions, power, pleasure, security, race, nation, or class some kind of absolute importance. Projections of this kind can be brutally naive. Or they may be culturally sophisticated. But whatever the form they take, they all end in self-destruction and the sacrifice of others. An individual or even a whole culture eventually sacrifices its own humanity to an all-demanding idol. Victimization of the weak, prejudice, envy, and greed are, all alike, the unholy result of minds and hearts skewed away from our common destiny in God. We lose our souls when our sense of self becomes numbed in its primary relationships to God, to society, and to the rest of creation. With the idols on the outside demanding all our exclusive attention and with the demons from within driving us in a hard, narrow rut of obsessions, it is little wonder that the human spirit has no room to expand into the universe of love and compassion.

In contrast, the Holy Spirit inspires the works of reconciliation, hope, and healing. God's Spirit opens a space for a healthy proportion, right relationships, and creative freedom: "The fruit of the Spirit is love, joy, peace, patience, kindness, generosity, faithfulness, gentleness, and self-control. There is no law against such things" (Gal 5:22-23). The holiness of the divine Spirit manifests itself in the great values without which the progress of any culture would be impossible. Such holiness is both healing and whole making. It leads to peace where before there was anger, conflict, and violence. It inspires patience and forgiveness where before there was resentment, vindictiveness, and isolation. Self-absorption and self-indulgence are replaced by self-sacrificing, other-regarding love. The "Lord, the giver of life" is the inexhaustible divine Gift of forgiveness and new beginnings.

VIII

Through the Spirit's inspiration, the Old and New Testaments make up the one book, the Bible of the church's Sacred Scriptures. This one "in-Spirited" book of faith and revelation is the Spirit's gift to all believers. Israel and the church are thus scripturally and "Spirit-ually" related. The health of this relationship derives from the Holy Spirit as the inspiring force working in all the expressions of faith through the ages (see 1 Pet 1:10-12).

More to the point, the Spirit of the Father and the Son is given to overcome the inertia of the past. The coming of the Spirit counters the tendency to bolster our present security by endlessly recalling the past as a golden age. In that fantasy, the ways of God were always clear and the people of God were all saints. But in fact, then and now, life was never a tranquil repetition of what had always been. Life is always moving on in ways beyond human calculation, defeating every effort to recover the past. But when the living stream of the Spirit begins to flow, reality can no more be reduced to a repetition of what has been. It is not a matter of recovering what once was. When the Spirit moves in the free air of the kingdom of God, it impels believers to move into the future—out of which God is coming to meet us. It does not permit any return to an untroubled existence. In New Testament terms, this unsettling Spirit occasions scandal by guiding Peter to the house of the pagan Cornelius (Acts 11). It surprises the early community with the unsettling gift of the former persecutor Paul (Acts 9:13-15). It is the advantage that comes upon the departure of the earthly Jesus (John 16:7). It leads to a knowledge of things that before could not be borne (John 16:12-13). The symbol of the Spirit works in the imagination of Christian faith to open it to the unimaginably new—as when St. Augustine in his *Confessions* (1.27) speaks of his experience of a "beauty ever ancient and ever new."

It is customary in Christian language to speak of the community made one "in the unity of the Holy Spirit." Such unity, however, does not mean merging into God so as to lose one's own identity. Nor does such unity suggest a monochrome uniformity among the children of the Father. The gift of the Spirit brings about unity-in-distinction. This Holy Breath animates a community of distinct persons (1 Cor 12:12-30). The powerful coming of the Holy Spirit at Pentecost enabled communication in the different languages of the known world (Acts 2:5-12). His presence inspires mutual belonging and collaboration in a variety of gifts given for the achievement of the common good (1 Cor 12:7)—one Body of Christ with its different members manifesting the grace of the Spirit for the good of all. While the unity of the Spirit abolishes differences in race, religion, social status, and gender, it does this only as much as such differences cause unredeemed isolation, envy, and aggression. It does not preclude the potential of such differences to be gifts in the one body of believers. In the Spirit that comes from the Father, there is room for difference and room for the surprise of the new. In the Father's house, there are many rooms (John 14:2).

In confessing the Mother of Christ as "the Virgin Mary," the Creed invites us to adore the Spirit and the unique capacity of the divine freedom to bring forth the new. It culminates in the Word made flesh, born of the Virgin Mary. This aspect of Christian faith brings home to us that the genesis of the divine Word in the human world is outside the genetic capacity of any created process. The Word made flesh is not a product of nature but the revelation of the mysterious workings of the Spirit. When Love comes to dwell with us, it transforms all it touches.

Still, God has chosen a human cooperator: Mary, from whom Jesus is born. Inspired by the Spirit, her faith defines her being. She is pure receptivity to the Spirit, pure attention to the Word, pure adoration of the Father: "For the Mighty One has done great things for me" (Luke 1:49). She is defined in no other way and by no other relationship—neither by a human partner nor by social expectations. What determines her existence is solely what God can be and what God can do; she is characterized by who God is for her and by who she is for God. She is the woman who most intimately knows that "for nothing will be impossible with God" (Luke 1:37). In her faithful existence is inscribed the conviction that the gift of God is given out of divine freedom, not as a result of human merit or ambition or natural development. In her, the Spirit's divine freedom communicates with a created freedom. Divine Love calls for a human love to be its partner in the world's transformation.

The meaning of Mary's virginity implies neither a glorification nor a demeaning of human sexuality. What it does express is the divine freedom of the Spirit working in creation. The Creed thus confesses the sheer grace of God, the divine ability to bring about a new creation in this woman. There is, as all human beings know, a wondrous intimacy and generativity in the eros of human love. But such a familiar form of love does not simply bring God down from heaven to make the mystery of God either our instrument or our property. God comes because God gives. And God gives because God freely loves and chooses to do so. And in choosing to do so, the Spirit of God inspires a freedom in the other, the Virgin Mary, to receive and cooperate.

The Blessed Virgin is invoked only in the community faith as it is guided by the Spirit. Outside of the mystery enveloping her, she cannot be known. Consequently, her virginity has meaning only within the universe of grace. At this point, faith must learn its own reserve. There is no place for any form of theological voyeurism in a vain effort to reduce God's impossible ways to the humanly familiar. Indeed, the virginal vocation of Mary becomes apparent only in the light of the resurrection of the Son and in the outpouring of the Spirit. It belongs to a new language of the world's transformation in Christ. Love has broken through as the sovereign power at work in the universe, transforming all it touches.

In that light, faith turns to Mary. She stands with the disciples at Pentecost in her unique role in the mystery of Christ and in the outpouring of the Spirit. In her virginity is embodied the intensity of surrender to the Spirit now demanded of all believers. By acknowledging her virginity, faith reaches a point of its deliberately not knowing the mystery. At that point, the utter freedom of the Holy Spirit is acknowledged. Through the Spirit of God comes the impossibly gracious gift we most need. And yet it remains outside our control, our comprehension, and our merits. At such a limit, the virginity of Mary is an icon of the divine Spirit, not a sign of human self-abnegation.

These different lines of convergence on the gift of the Holy Spirit lead to a central point. The eternal Spirit of Love uniting the Father and the Son is poured out on all creation and works in the whole church to awaken us to true life. Through the Spirit, faith comes to a deep union with Christ and to an intimate relationship with the Father, and it expands into a growing community of love and life.

CHAPTER 7

The Church: Love Formed in History

The one God is a communion of love and life. This divine community of the three Divine Persons opens out to enfold into itself all who receive the gift of God. And so the church comes into being. Through its faith, hope, and love, the gathering of the faithful is already participating in the divine vitality. At every moment of its journey through history, the church is overhearing, as it were, the prayer of Jesus to the Father:

> The glory that you have given me I have given them, so that they may be one, as we are one, I in them and you in me, that they may be completely one. (John 17:22-23)

In this hope, the church is that part of the world that has awakened to the eternal Love at work in all creation and in all hearts. Love forms in the drama of history a community witnessing to the great mystery that has revealed itself and continues to prove itself from generation to generation. The people of God, whether they be saints or sinners, have found the promise of eternal life in the God who "so loved the world" (John 3:16).

I

So closely are the church's story and the story of Jesus intertwined that one of the most treasured biblical descriptions of the church is "the Body of Christ." Each member of the church is united to him as the head and animated by his Spirit. Through the inspired Scriptures and its sacraments of grace, the church nourishes its members with the life-giving reality of Christ and energizes them with his Holy Spirit. In this way, the deep life of the church pulses with the Love-life of the Trinity itself. It lives from the all-holy mystery of God turned toward the world in love.

Though the church's deepest identity is founded in the mystery of Love, its human reality is obviously many-sided. Everything in the human world is marked with the ambiguity of failure, resistance, hesitations, confusion—and limitation. The church does not live above the human condition but is immersed in it. And yet, despite all the weaknesses of its human condition, its mission remains in every age to bring all peoples together, united in "one body and one Spirit, . . . one hope . . . , one Lord, one faith, one baptism, one God and Father of all, who is above all and though all and in all" (Eph 4:4-6).

The dream of unity in love is too often interrupted by the nightmare of hatred and divisions. At such times, the church must confront the cold reality of a world still far from Christ and closed against the fullness of life he offers. The pilgrim church is ever "on the way," journeying through time to the City of God. We members of the church begin all liturgical acts by confessing our sinfulness and asking for pardon. Such a confession amounts to saying, "Don't look only at the scandal of our individual or collective faults and failings; look at the Love that has found us, that is always offering mercy, always inspiring a more genuine love in return."

II

The story of the church will only be fully told in the light of God's fullest self-revelation as Love. In the meantime, as the people of God move along their pilgrim path, there are at least four other stories that give a sense of identity and direction for all.

First, there is the story of Mary. She is the one who says "Yes!" to the mystery of God's love with the whole power of her being. And so she becomes the Mother of Jesus, the Mother of Christ, the Mother of God-with-us: "Here am I, the servant of the Lord; let it be with me according to your word" (Luke 1:38). In her perfect receptivity to God's love, she shows us what the church is meant to be: a mother bringing Christ to birth in all peoples and in every human being. For this reason, the church finds in Mary the special symbol of its identity.

Second, there is Peter, "the rock" on which Jesus builds his church (Matt 16:18). Despite his human weakness, even to the point of denying Christ, Peter is given the task of organizing the church in the world, to hold it together, to strengthen the faith of others, and to supervise its growth. If Our Lady, "the Mother of the Church," always stands for the mystery of God's grace from which the church comes, Peter embodies the power of this Love to call forth a visible organization. There emerges a living, recognizable reality in the world of time and space. Despite all the failures, ambiguity, and incompleteness of our lives, the church takes shape to act and suffer in the world of human realities.

Third, there is John, as well as the "the Beloved Disciple" of his gospel. His story is always expressed in terms of intimate love for Christ and those whom the Lord loves. He emphasizes the new commandment to love one another as Christ has loved us. The decisive reality for John is the mystery of God's original love, received and lived as the deepest form of life: "By this everyone will know that you are my disciples, if you have love one for another" (John 13:35). The church, consequently, finds its identity concentrated in the mystery of Love: "Beloved, let us love one another, because love is from God; everyone who loves is born of God and knows God" (1 John 4:7). For that reason, John tells of the Lord asking Peter three times, "Do you love me?" (John 21:15-17). From that love flows the authority to feed the lambs and sheep of Christ's flock.

Fourth, our sense of the church would not be complete without the story of Paul. It is the story of extraordinary conversion: the grace of God transforms this former persecutor of the church into the greatest proclaimer of Christ. The result was that his preaching centered on the utter generosity of God and on the necessity we are under to rely on God's sheer grace above all else. God's gift is not tied to merit, virtue, or legal purity. It is utterly free, made out of sheer goodness, and discloses an unimaginable generosity. Thus, Paul stands in the church as a witness to the ever-surprising power of the Spirit to lead us to Christ, "in whom are hidden all the treasures of wisdom and knowledge" (Col 2:3).

We could, of course, add the stories of many others—those of the apostles and saints, teachers and martyrs and mystics, religious founders and reformers. But these all keep coming back to the telling the story of Love. It has appeared in Christ Jesus as a mystery to be received (Mary). It is a way of life and community that has taken shape in human history (Peter). It is Love that has overflowed into innumerable loving lives (John). It has come as "amazing grace," ever surprising us with its power (Paul).

The Love that has revealed itself and has found each one of us has placed us in good company. We are part of a communion of brothers and sisters, each beloved in the sight of God. None of us can say, "I believe" in Christ apart from the "we believe" of the immense community of Christian believers, stretching from the past into the present and then into an incalculable future.

III

One of the oldest symbolic descriptions of the community of faith is "Holy Mother Church." She, the church, is a great womb of life from which each of us is born into life in Christ, made a member of the family of God, and breathes the Holy "Breath" of the Spirit. The church forms us as Christians. As the matrix of our life in Christ, it communicates that life to us in its Scriptures, sacraments, and manifold witnesses. It challenges us to a deeper conversion and supports all the variety of vocations that make up the Christian community. As it embodies and communicates the unfailing love of God, the church shows a special patience with each of us. Holy Mother Church never loses hope for us, no matter how sorry our performance or how weak our faith might be. It is with us, through life and death, in a way that no other earthly institution could pretend to be.

On the other hand, it is not as though we are being given a free ride in a vast impersonal institution that came before us and will survive after us. If it is true that the fundamental ministry of the church is to form us as Christians, there comes a point when we are called, in the maturity of faith, to form and even re-form the church from generation to generation. After all, the church is made up of people like us who share a common faith, hope, and love. Yet there is a variety of responsibilities and a rich range of gifts in those who make up the church at any time. Each of us is called to be a "church maker" and to make a unique contribution to the life of that church, for each person is equipped with special God-given gifts (1 Cor 12:4-26). These gifts of the Spirit are all connected with serving the community, witnessing to Christ, and proclaiming the Gospel. It is the vocation of all Christians to become seeds of the church in their time and culture. We are meant to be not passengers complaining about the ride but brothers and sisters in the one great community project of life to the full, open to all.

Each of us is called to share in the mission of the church to evangelize the world. In this respect, we are all both responsible *to* the church and responsible *for* it. This kind of twofold responsibility results from our being caught up in the church's God-given mission. If the church is to be true to itself, it must always be pointing beyond itself. As a community of faith it is essentially an open circle, opening out beyond its present boundaries toward the whole of humanity and all creation. Indeed, the church is that part of humanity and that part of the world that has come alive to the all-inclusive love of God. The all-embracing character of Love inspires the outreach of mission. The will of God is experienced as an impulse to go beyond what the church is at any given time to an open-ended future beholden only to the universal reach of God's healing and transforming love.

The church, then, is the historically identifiable embodiment and manifestation of God's self-giving love. Participating in this vast community of mutual love and shared mission, each member of the church is called to live a love that "bears all things, believes all things, hope all things, endures all things" (1 Cor 13:7). As each is a member of Christ, all share his Spirit and are promised an enjoyment of those "fruits of the Spirit" that St. Paul lists as "love, joy, peace, patience, kindness, generosity, faithfulness, gentleness, and self-control" (Gal 5:22-23).

The gathering of believers, identified by their celebration of baptism and the Eucharist, is sent into the world with its own distinctive mission. It thus continues the mission that Jesus himself has received from the Father (John 20:21). The Love that is the object of Christian witness looks to its practical realization in the community and through the mission of the church to the world. As the unity of believers participates in the all-embracing unity of the Father and the Son, it witnesses to the world the Love that has been made known (John 17:23, 26). The Christian community, therefore, and the community of communities that is the church, exists in the world that is the object of God's love (John 3:16). To repeat: the church is that part of that world which has come alive to the extent of God's gift.

IV

As Father, primordial Love unreservedly gave itself in the crucified and risen Son. It continues to be communicated in the Spirit and is humanly materialized in the body of believers, the church. As a communion of faith, the church draws its life from the Love-life of the Trinity itself. Its mission is likewise inspired by the boundless generosity of Love. It consists in reaching beyond itself to evangelize the nations. It is thus an instrument for the realization of God's universal reign. In this way, the church is that part of the world already wakened to the glory of Christ's saving grace.

The *we* of the church exists as an open circle. It is peopled by those "made one by the unity of the Father, the Son and the holy Spirit," in the words of St. Cyprian (cited in *Lumen Gentium* 4). This *we* can never be closed in on itself; for it lives within the all-inclusive range of both the incarnation and the outpouring of the Spirit—so that God might be "all in all" (1 Cor 15:28). This *we*, in its receptivity to Love, must keep expanding through the course of history to include generations yet to be born.

Implicit in all Christian doctrines is the story of God's self-giving love. The church is the historical telling point where such a story is told and heard. In the church, the incarnation of the Word and the gift of the Spirit come together in the flesh-and-blood reality of human beings witnessing to their faith. When describing its identity and mission, Catholic tradition uses the four words: *one, holy, catholic,* and *apostolic*. What follows is a brief remark on each of them.

ONE

The church's oneness derives from the unity of the trinitarian God. It is called to stand in history as a sign and agent of this unity-in-love.

In this regard, the fundamental dynamic of Christian community can be described in terms of unification. It is centripetal: the church must become one in seeking to live from its center, Christ, and so overcome the divisions within it. It is centrifugal, too, in that the unity of the church is continuously extended outward. It seeks to invite all the nations and peoples of the world into the unity of the Holy Spirit. Here the church embodies Christ's prayer for unity in a twofold manner. First, the church exists as one because that prayer has been answered. Second, believers must keep on praying and working that the prayer of Jesus will be answered in all its fullness: "Holy Father, protect them in your name that you have given me, so that they may be one, as we are one" (John 17:11). The prayer of Jesus opens onto history of the successive ages of faith:

> I ask not only on behalf of these, but also on behalf of those who will believe in me through their word, that they may all be one. As you, Father, are in me and I am in you, may they also be in us, so that the world may believe that you have sent me. (John 17:20-22)

A sense of the one unifying mystery of Love pervades every aspect of ecclesial consciousness. Love summons the faithful into union with Christ. It breathes into all the members of the Body of Christ the one Spirit of life and love. Love is named in the trinitarian invocation of our baptism. It is expressed in our shared vocation and hope. It looks to the whole of creation transformed and to the life of the world to come. Love works in its every dimension:

> There is one body and one Spirit, just as you were called to one hope of your calling, one Lord, one faith, one baptism, one God and Father of all, who is above all and through all and in all. (Eph 4:4-6)

Needless to say, such a vision of unity inspires an unstinted working for unity through a serious ecumenical commitment. The unity that the church embodies and believes flows from the trinitarian heart of Love. It overflows into a unifying and reconciling action. How the unity of all in Christ will be achieved, and when it will be brought about, are questions only answered in the future to which the Spirit leads. But there is no ambiguity attached to the imperatives of unity. Reconciliation, dialogue, shared prayer, and collaborative action are inescapable imperatives. Unless the unity of the church is a living and unifying force, it becomes an ideology of exclusion. It would not promise healing and reconciliation in Christ but become a cause of conflict and decomposition.

Holy

Despite the obvious limitations and even scandals of the observable Christian community, Christian faith expresses belief in the church as holy. Here it is a matter of adoring, in humility and hope, the reality of the Holy Spirit working within the church. For the church is fundamentally holy only because God is holy. At the depths of its life, the church inhales and breathes forth the Holy Breath of the Father and the Son. Such holiness does not fail: it is the inexhaustible source of the church's grace. The purifying, healing, and transforming love of God is active at every moment.

The holiness of the church never simply resides in the sum total of its holy members, even of the saints in its midst. The gift of God's love is an unfailing principle of holiness. It is ever being given; it is present and preceding any human response. When the church expresses faith in her own holiness, such a confession is not an act of self-congratulation on attaining some level of spiritual, ethical, or mystical excellence. It is simply the humble confession of gratitude for the gift that has been made. Thankfulness abounds as the gift keeps on being made. Despite the vicissitudes and fragility of our history, God's love is without end. As receptive to the gracious holiness of God, the church lives her life by "abounding in thanksgiving" (Col 2:7). Secure in the conviction that her holiness is a pure gift, the church—in all her members—is freed to confess her sinfulness. The conscience of the church stirs with a summons to the ever more radical demands of conversion to the Love that is her origin and destiny.

In short, the God-given holiness of the church is accessible only to faith that receives the gift of God's love. Such holiness is not somehow contained by the religious institution, nor is it a spiritual accomplishment. It is a gift that keeps on being unreservedly offered. Christ is risen, and the Spirit has been given.

Admittedly, belief in the one *holy* church is an especially contentious issue today. Never before has the vast historical reality of Christianity been studied in all the light and darkness of the different eras of its two-thousand-year history. Many are disillusioned in the face of the human imperfection that is all too visible. The historical weight of the church seems too heavy a burden for faith to bear. We are tempted to disencumber our personal faith of such an incubus of scandal, conflict, and confusion. Standing back from everything that is commonly termed "the institutional church" is a more spiritually comforting posture. Hence, there is heard the familiar refrain, "Jesus, Yes! The church, No!"

There was an ancient heresy that recoiled from accepting the full humanity of Jesus. It held that he, because he was divine, could only appear to be human. This heresy is known as Docetism (from the Greek *dokein*, "to appear"). Today, we might ask ourselves whether we still tend to be docetic, not only in regard to the genuine humanity of Jesus but also in our appreciation of the historical humanity of the church—and even of the human reality of ourselves. Some aspire to a pure, immediate union with God and Christ without any messy mediation on the part of a sinful church. That may well be an exalted spiritual aspiration. But genuine faith has a firmer grip on reality. It recognizes that it is only in the church, through the often ambiguous reality of the words and deeds of very human fellow Christians, that we have come to know Christ. Only through the familiar realities of bread and wine do we eat and drink his reality in the Eucharist. Only in the company of believers do we receive his Spirit and hear the Word in all the inflections of human speech. Only through the authority and discernment of the church do we accept this particular collection of ancient documents written in extinct languages as the inspired Scriptures.

Scandals can be met with an extreme reaction. There can also be an impatient demand for something better, wiser, more inspired, and more humane. When demands or aspirations of this kind are pushed to extremes, a particular like-minded group—or, for that matter, any individual—can, in effect, "excommunicate" the larger church. If that is the case, the reality of the church's holiness cannot but be overlooked. It is possible to be censoriously fixated on some real or supposed instance of failure and sinfulness in a particular situation. If that is the case, it is possible to wonder whether those most scandalized and judgmental are trying to find an excuse for not being involved in the flesh-and-blood history of real human beings and of the church they belong to. That has its demands, its risks, and its ambiguities. Some can conveniently hide from participating in the reality of church life by projecting standards of unliveable excellence onto their fellow Christians and the church organizations that serve them.

There are serious questions to be asked. Is our capacity to be scandalized all too convenient? Are we inventing a private version of self-justifying sanctity so as not to belong to the corporate, pilgrim existence of the church? In the end, are we in fact living *off* the church in fear of a commitment to live *for* and *in* it? Might not the grace of God be in fact humanly present in our midst and yet beyond the perception of those who so harshly judge? They may be blinkered by their rigid, narrowly individual criteria. It might be that a prim, bloodless judgmentalism can make us blind to real holiness. More deeply, can we ever know what we do not truly love?

Of course, it is not all shrouded in ambiguity. There are always in the midst of the Christian community those who have received the mystery of holiness into their lives. Such as these challenge routines and compromises of our religious "business as usual." These saints and martyrs, confessors and mystics, religious founders and reformers, pastors and prophets show a far more imaginative generosity. That is not to forget the millions of good people, across the generations, for whom there is no special name. Without resentment or disgust, they live a holiness that cannot be appreciated by the scandalized, the disaffected, and the threatened. Not to recognize this holy company and the Holy Spirit of Love at work in all lives must mean that the true holiness of the church disappears from view. In the meantime, the church is here. It is populated by real human beings, sinners and saints. It is masked with ambiguities, and yet it confesses its sins. All the while, the church offers to all, throughout life and in death, the fullness of Christ.

Through the ministry of the church, God's boundless gift of Love is still offering itself. It invites a more wholehearted participation and a more heartfelt response. Even the most generous love for God can discover new depths and a wider scope. The most generous service is keenly aware of what still needs to be done.

CATHOLIC

"Catholic" derives from the Greek adjective *katholikos*, meaning "all-inclusive," and the adverb *kat'holou*, "regarding the whole," "open to the whole." It contrasts with the sectarian and exclusive *haeresis*, "heresy." This distortion occurs when holding to some part of Christian belief distorts a sense of the whole. A sense of proportion suffers. Traditionally, Christian language spoke of "the Catholic faith" (*fides catholica*), or "the Catholic Church" (*ecclesia catholica*). "Catholicity" denoted a quality essential to the faith of a historical community of Christian believers. But "Catholicism," like all "-ism" words, can be misused to suggest the ideology of a closed system. In that case, the proponents or victims of a narrow, ideological religious system should be called not "Catholics" but "Catholicists"! The recent history of the Catholic Church might be best understood as a movement of conversion—away from a defensive "Catholicist" exclusivism to a living catholicity of dialogue and communion. The movement toward a reconciling, dialogical manner of being the church makes us ask, What does authentic catholicity mean for the church? What does it imply, and what does it demand?

Being "catholic" implies being open to God's love embracing all peoples and cultures and epochs. It means that the church must share in the catholicity of trinitarian love. This reality of such love is originally manifested by the one God, the maker of "all that is." The Father gives what is most intimate to himself for the world's salvation: "For God so loved the *world* that he gave his only Son" (John 3:16; emphasis added). By receiving such a gift, the catholicity of the church expands to a universe of connections centered in him through whom *all* things were made. It is open to the life-giving Spirit who has spoken through the prophets. It adores the power of this Spirit working in Jesus as he was born of the Virgin Mary and raised from the dead. In acknowledging that the Holy Spirit has been poured out on all the earth, catholicity is an ever-expanding consciousness. It is bounded only by the limitless love of God at work in every moment of history and in every atom of the universe.

Despite schisms and divisions, a new age of ecumenism is now occurring; and every Christian community now has its own distinctive responsibility to maintain a more dynamic catholicity. The church can never rest content with its catholicity at any stage. It is an open movement, finding its essential expression in the outreach and welcome of reconciliation and dialogue.

Further, Catholics of the North (Europe and North America) are now faced with the new huge demographic shift in church membership toward the southern regions of the globe. That is where

70 percent of Catholics now live. This new situation in Africa, Asia, Oceania, and South America contrasts on many points with that of the North. The populations are much younger and, in some cases (Asia, Aboriginal Australia), the cultures are much older than those of Europe. Certainly, as in India and Africa, they are more religious compared to the secularism of the North. Politically speaking, these southern regions are postcolonial. As a consequence, they are inevitably embroiled in the dramas of self-determination. Apart from being racially nonwhite (a factor contributing to the dramatic "otherness" of the emerging church), these regions are economically poorer and structurally disadvantaged in the transnational organization of the global economy.

The church cannot but recognize the need for a larger catholicity in terms of culture, demography, and economic justice. But there is a further, more subversive imperative. It gives expression to the catholicity of Love. It looks to affect all human relationships in the individual, social, and political spheres of life. Patriarchal, monarchical, feudal, and sexist modes of relationships have in fact influenced much of the church's history. Christian conscience has been awakened in this era and challenged to become more inclusive, democratic, and interactive in its communication. The catholicity of Love "from above" inspires new healing forms of catholicity "from below" as the one global world of our humanity emerges.

The catholicity of the church is intrinsically diminished if its faith and hope do not embrace the wonder of the universe itself. The time of the church is a microsecond at the end of billions of years of cosmic history. A living catholicity demands that faith remember such a past. Christian believers cannot but adore the creative providence that has brought us to this point and now takes us beyond it. If we believe that "through him all things were made," then the meaning of catholicity is to provoke a humble exploration of "all things" making up the universe. For instance, Christian faith can open out to a more reverent dialogue with the scientific exploration of the wonder and immensity of the cosmos.

APOSTOLIC

In its apostolic character, the church participates in the outgoing scope of God's love in Christ. As *apostolos* in the Greek suggests, to be an apostle is to be given a mission. One is "sent out" as the bearer of good tidings. So sent by the Father, the Son is the "apostle" par excellence. To believe in him is to enter into his life of mission. Christ commissions the church to carry on, and to carry out, what was begun in him. In his prayer to the Father, Jesus prays, "As you have sent me into the world, so I have sent them into the world" (John 17:18). The sending goes on. It reaches into history from beyond history to involve the church of every present in the mission of Christ. The eternal Now of God's saving love connects the church with its apostolic past and now sends Christians into times and situations just as alien and threatening as anything the original apostles had to face.

In its apostolic character, the church is turned out of itself toward the world and its hopes. Those sitting in the shadow of death where the light does not yet shine may well stop us with questions such as "Where are you, where is this church, as we strain to hear any words of light and life? Why has your Good News been so long coming to us?" Believers may well recoil from the enormity of the task. The future is a prospect for which there are so few signposts. And yet the Christian mission is one of hope since it witnesses to the inexhaustible energies of God's love. In the power of the Holy Spirit, we are sent out to take our place in the apostolic mission of the church, just as the whole church participates in the mission of Christ himself. The command of Christ continues to resonate in her life:

> Go therefore and make disciples of all nations, baptizing them in the name of the Father and of the Son and of the Holy Spirit, and teaching them to obey everything that I have commanded you. And remember, I am with you always, to the end of the age." (Matt 28:19-20)

With such a commission, Christians today can profitably recall the varieties of apostolic witness recorded in their past. We have already mentioned Mary, in the virginal totality of her faith, surrendering herself to the incarnate mystery of her Son. We have made frequent reference to the early Johannine communities of believers who found their center in the great affirmation "God is Love" and who came to the practical realization that this kind of love had to be lived if God was to be known. For his part, Paul is the living witness to the capacities of divine grace to convert and transform us in heart and mind to life in Christ. Then, the apostle Peter, the leader of the Twelve, was sent to confirm the faith of his brothers and sisters by so forming the church that it could preserve the integrity of faith in the midst of an ambiguous world: "You are Peter, and on this rock I will build my church, and the gates of Hades will not prevail against it" (Matt 16:18). Each of these kinds of apostolic witness continues into the present. They call on each generation of believers to put a whole life into the cause of Christ and his Gospel.

The church continues to be sent into the whole world, with all the different epochs and cultures evident in human history. So sent into such a world, the church can never be a tranquil sect living outside of time or aloof from the drama of history. The apostolic church can never rest where it is. It is always being sent out and sent on, as well as sent into places it may well fear to go. But the insistent universality of God's grace provokes Christians of every age to a more courageous, more inventive apostolic witness. For the Gospel is always to be proclaimed within the inconclusive unfolding of human history. Those who receive it with purity of heart become, in their turn, witnesses to the life-giving Love embodied in Christ. If the church and every Christian within it are "apostolic," then all must share in the patience of God. Love alone has time for all, over all epochs and in all cultures, until that prayer is answered, "that they may be one" (John 17:11).

Love brings about its own kind of radical liberation. No one's existence is to be defined by evils committed or suffered. Nor is the story of life to be reduced to a summary of failures. The Love that has been there from the beginning continues to offer a new beginning for all who have sinned, failed, and lost their way. The words of the risen One, addressed to disciples who knew the guilt in abandoning him, are instructive for his followers in every age: "Peace be with you. . . . Receive the Holy Spirit. If you forgive the sins or any, they are forgiven them" (John 20:21-23). The holiness of the Spirit, not the guilt of sin, is the defining factor in all lives.

A big question is heard today: How is belonging to the church compatible with a personal spirituality? "Spirituality" can seem to imply an almost automatic rejection of the "institutional church." When the church is viewed as an extreme example of "organized religion," it appears in sorry contrast to a "customized" spirituality. The institutional church is deemed to lack the qualities of inwardness, liberation, creativity, and flexibility. Consequently, the image of the church is loaded with negative associations. Well-intentioned people could be excused for thinking that the integrity of Christian faith is to be found not in the church but outside it, despite any form of belonging to it. The strong presumption is that free-ranging, highly personalized spirituality is always being compromised by "the structures." The free spirit cannot be burdened with the weight of the tradition of faith and morality that informs the corporate life of the historical church. To be truly spiritual is to be disencumbered of all this.

It happens, then, that suspicion of the church is so ingrained that the possibility of anyone finding peace and inspiration as a member of the church is hardly recognized. In such a perspective, it seems that the church is located outside the sphere of spirituality altogether as an alien and external organization. But there is a larger view. As already emphasized, the church is that identifiable part of the world that cultivates an explicit awareness of the universal mystery of Love at work. If that larger vision is lost, any effort to understand the reality of the church is easily reduced to a sociological analysis of only its most imperfect and limited institutional form. Yet to a genuine Christian vision from within, the identity of the church flows from the trinitarian life and love of God. That transcendent reality is the source, sustenance, and goal of all that the church is, in its deepest communal life and in its visible organization.

When the church ceases to be located within the mystery of God's self-giving love, inevitable distortions result. Ecclesiastical preoccupations in regard to policies, appointments, procedures, and politics take over. Organizational problems overwhelm any sense of mystery. The sense of communion in Christ and of Spirit-empowered mission is pushed to the edges. Scandals, problems, and partisan conflicts take up so much time and energy of Christian life that a question is commonly heard: Why stay in the church? But the right question, even if it tends to shock our present presuppositions, is this: Why does the church continue to have patience with us sinners, given the often pitiful level of our Christian witness? We can never hope to understand the church unless we commit ourselves to it. In that commitment, thanksgiving and humility and conversion play their role in interpreting what is really going on in the life of the people of God.

The institutional shape of the church is never perfect, and it never will be. But that institutional component is necessary. If Christian witness is to have a presence and a voice in the groaning, conflicted reality of world history, it must have a visible organization. The Christian community has to confront huge antagonistic forces that have no reservations when it comes to assuming an institutional form: capitalism, Marxism, militarism, racism, and institutionalized prejudice of all kinds. Add to these the unsleeping enterprise of the commercial and advertising institutions that drive mass consumer culture—"the opium of the people" beyond anything Marx could have imagined. Put all such "institutions" in the context of the institutional media—often owned and directed by any and all of the above—and one might ask why the church and Christian people generally are not far more organized in order to have a more effective institutional presence in society. It would serve the antihuman institutions rather well if the church opted for a pure spirituality as it is often understood. The First Letter of John ends with the counsel, "Little children, keep yourselves from idols" (1 John 5:21). If such words are to mean more than an invisible, interior attitude, they must presuppose some form of institutional resistance to the idols of the day. That in turn would mean "instituting" a clear space where God is adored and the Body of Christ is formed and nourished. It would mean that the church must take its place in history and culture.

In its historical embodiment, the institution of the church protects the spirituality that is otherwise struggling for expression in any culture. The church does what spirituality alone cannot do. It confronts the violent antihuman realities of the world, even if this means that the church itself is often wounded in the process. Moreover, the church is the bearer of millennial traditions of doctrine, liturgy, and Christian witness centered on the great affirmation "God is Love." All its particular spiritualities—for example, Benedictine,

Carmelite, Franciscan, Jesuit, and, more recently, "lay," to name but a few—exhibit a demanding asceticism. The people of God are not without their prophets, martyrs, founders, and reformers.

Believers need continuous personal conversion, and the institutional dimension of the Christian community is always in need of reform. The church must be transparent in its witness. The mystery of Love that is at its heart must be made quite clear, both to those on the inside and to those on the outside. Those inside the community of faith can feel disoriented and confused in their Christian lives. For them it is time for a deep re-centering of their beliefs and devotions in the Love that God is. Those outside the Christian community are representatives of "the world" to be evangelized by the church. For most, the church, for good or ill, is an undeniable presence in Western history (at least). But could these people possibly imagine that this church exists only to draw them into the realm of love, mercy, and the promise of eternal life? However that question is to be answered, it is not the time for members of the church to lose heart. Faith is living from the love that wells up in the heart of God. The radical simplicity of Christian life is to live a love that "bears all things, believes all things, hope all things, endures all things" (1 Cor 13:7). That is what it means to be the church in the world, in any and every age.

CHAPTER 8

Eternal Life: Love Consummated

 "God is Love" is the last word on Christian existence. The six terms already explored are signposts directing us to this conclusion—the culmination of "the breadth and length and height and depth" (Eph 3:18) of the Love that has been revealed. Love keeps on being Love and looks to its ultimate consummation when God will be "all in all" (1 Cor 15:27).

I

God's love promises eternal life. The stream of life without end has already begun to flow, even if it is often hidden beneath the ambiguities of our present form of life. But already we enjoy the pledge and promise of future glory and look to the joy of a final gift. God's will to bring us to life *will* be done. Love will not be patient forever with the flickering inconclusiveness of earthly life. What awaits us has already irrupted in the resurrection of the Crucified, and in the outpouring of the Spirit.

Love gives life. As "the resurrection and the life" (John 11:25), Jesus communicates the fullness of life in God. Life to the full consists of loving union with Christ himself and with the Father who sent his Son into the world for its salvation: "And this is eternal life, that they may know you, the only true God, and Jesus Christ whom you have sent" (John 17:3). Faith continues to long for its fulfillment, and love desires its consummation in the "the life of the world to come." But that life has already come into this world (John 1:4). In this respect, the resurrection of the dead is not strictly an "afterlife" as far as our basic relationship to God is concerned. Love's crowning gift of life without end will be the radiance and completion of what has already begun within us. Christian speech appeals to many images when referring to the final fulfillment of life in God. However hidden such life might be in the rough fabric of our present existence, it cannot be thought of except as the blossoming forth of the relationships we already have with the God who has first loved us (1 John 4:10). John's letter catches the sense of present actuality, of hiddenness, and of promised fulfillment:

> Beloved, we are God's children now; what we will be has not yet been revealed. What we do know is this: when he is revealed, we will be like him, for we will see him as he is. (1 John 3:2)

All the gifts that flow from Love promise completion. The peace that the world cannot give (John 14:27) grows. Faith already stirs with a sense of the final delight of that joy which no one can take from us (John 15:12; 16:24). The truth will finally set us free (John 8:32) in the plenitude of the abundant life that Jesus came to give (John 10:10). A boundless love will reveal itself as the power that nothing in all creation can resist. The dark night of faith looks to the dawn of its final day.

II

Already we are the children of God (1 John 3:2). However, the groaning ambiguities and tensions of this present existence remain. In Paul's idiom, the outward "groaning" of creation and the inward "groanings" of the Christian are supported by the deepest "groanings" of the Spirit, in expectation of the fullness of revelation: "In hope we were saved. . . . We wait for it with patience" (Rom 8:24-25). At present, hope can claim only the first fruits of the Spirit. The full harvest is yet to ripen and be gathered.

All this is to say that the prayer of Jesus is still to be answered: "Father, I desire that those also, whom you have given me, may be with me where I am, to see my glory" (John 17:24). The world as loved by God (John 3:16) is the world into which Jesus has come as its savior (John 4:42; 1 John 2:2). Yet that world is yet to respond to the Love that has been shown it, "so that the world may believe that you have sent me" (John 17:21). Even though believers are already "God's children," it remains that "what we will be has not yet been revealed" (1 John 3:2).

The courage of faith is based in Jesus' victory over the world (John 16:33). It shows itself in a hope that this cosmic triumph will be fully displayed (1 John 5:4-5). The horizon of Christian life unfolds under the opened heaven, with "the angels of God ascending and descending upon the Son of Man" (John 1:51). Christ is the new Jacob's ladder of God's communication with us and of our communication with God. Nonetheless, the world as a whole has yet to lift its gaze to the glory that has been revealed. Only when the word of Jesus is fully kept will the love of the Father be manifest: "And we will come to them and make our home with them" (John 14:23). The final form of God's dwelling among us is strikingly expressed toward the end of the book of Revelation:

> See, the home of God is among mortals. He will dwell with them; they will be his people, and God himself will be with them; he will wipe every tear from their eyes. Death will be no more; mourning and crying and pain will be no more, for the first things have passed away. (Rev 21:3-4)

III

The corporate faith of the church envisions an ultimate communion in life beyond death. The Creed speaks of "the life of the world to come." Already in the light of Christ's resurrection, already enjoying the gift of his life-giving Spirit, the church anticipates its fulfillment. In what it already knows of God's love, Christian hope can use the defiant language of St. Paul in his certainty that "neither death, nor life, nor angels, nor rulers, nor things present, nor things to come, nor powers, nor height, nor depth, nor anything else in all creation, will be able to separate us from the love of God in Christ Jesus our Lord" (Rom 8:38-39).

In anticipation of the fulfillment of life in God, all believers already stand in communion with those who have gone before them. Though the dead are absent from this present life, they have died into life's ultimate mystery, the true future of the world, "the life of the world to come." In the vitality of that holy communion—the communion of saints—the presence of the martyrs is of supreme importance. They witnessed to Christ unto death and suffered a violent removal from the world. But in the living community of grace and love they are given back to us. They are present to us in the Spirit, as witnesses to the Love that is stronger than any death we know. They are already living the fullness of life that the Spirit is nurturing within the lives of all the faithful despite the ambiguities and violence of this present time.

Hope looks forward to the resurrection of the dead and to the complete transformation of those who have died in faith. They are already incorporated in the risen Christ and, indeed, in the transformed universe that he embodies. The dead are not disincarnate souls, ethereal beings far less real than they were in life. The love of God has not ended merely in the production of shades and shadows of the real people who believed the Gospel. In the universe of Love's creation, all who die in Christ will be newly embodied as members of the Body of the risen One. As the bread and wine of the Eucharist become, through the power of the Spirit, our "true food and . . . true drink" (John 6:55), so our embodied existence is being brought to its fullest reality in a transformed world.

Looking toward the resurrection of the dead is the foundation of a sense of compassionate solidarity with the dead. The sober side of Christian realism is a humble admission that not all of us (any of us?) go into the presence of the Lord as wholly integrated into Christ and completely possessed by his Spirit. The perfect love that can cast out all fear is not yet our common possession. In all the variety of prayers for the dead, Christian tradition expresses total trust in the purifying power of Christ's love, along with a sense of solidarity with the human reality of the individuals we are. In that perspective of love and hope, death must be an event of judgment, purification, and final grace. It is the moment of truth.

At that point, we hitherto fragmented human beings will catch up with who we truly are. In a moment of perfect freedom we will be able to make an act of unreserved and unrestricted surrender to Christ. The doubts, hesitations, compromises, and distractions of our multilayered existence will then yield to a completed, integrated existence. We begin to burn, in the words of the great poem of St. John of Cross, as a "living flame of love." As the agent of that integration, the Holy Spirit of Love is like a purifying fire, purging all that we are in preparation for seeing God face to face.

A practical expression of belief in the resurrection of the dead is our praying for them. In Christ we stand with them. We are connected with them in the reality of what is occurring for all of us. For all are loved by God and feel the purifying and healing power of that love. The prayer of the church for the faithful departed is inspired by the all-merciful Spirit so that, as intercessors, we can be part of the final healing and liberation of all who have gone before us. In this solidarity of compassion, we belong together as recipients of God's mercy and forgiveness, as agents of reconciliation, and as praying for one another. Our prayers and love accompany the dead in their final transformation. Death does not break our communion with them. The love that the Spirit inspires reaches into death's darkness as a prayer: may those who have gone before us be given eternal rest, and may perpetual light shine upon them. The church enfolds each of the dying in the ancient prayer:

> Go forth, Christian soul, from this world,
> in the name of God the almighty Father,
> who created you,
> in the name of Jesus Christ, the Son of the living God,
> who suffered for you,
> in the name of the Holy Spirit,
> who was poured out upon you.
> Go forth, faithful Christian!
>
> May you live in peace this day,
> may your home be with God in Zion,
> with Mary, the virgin Mother of God,
> with Joseph, and all the angels and saints.[1]

Love's last word is an affirmation of life. In contrast to the mortality of earthly life, the decay that is inherent in our natural world, and the fragility and incompleteness of our lives within it, the world to come is the realm of life to the full. While "no eye has seen, nor ear heard, nor the human heart conceived, what God has prepared for those who love him" (1 Cor 2:9), Love is the very life of the new creation. For the destiny of creation is to be enfolded into the Love-life of the Trinity itself. Jesus prays to the Father for our inclusion in the fullness of this holy communion: "The glory that you have given me I have given them, so that they may be one, as we are one, I in them and you in me, that they may be completely one" (John 17:22-23).

The life of the world to come is already present as we participate in the activity of God's loving: "We know that we have passed from death to life because we love one another" (1 John 3:14). The love that has grown within us, the love that never ends (1 Cor 13:8), leads finally to its full evidence. The infinite light of God breaks into our being to give the "face-to-face" vision of God. The "beatific vision," as it has been traditionally termed, means that we shall meet God no longer through the limited intermediaries and mediations of this life but so as to receive into our hearts and minds the glory of the Light. But as the climax of our union with God, the vision of God face to face is also the culmination of God's communication to creation. As faith leads finally to its ultimate clarity and union with God, the original, self-giving, unconditional love of God for creation is achieved. It is the culminating moment when God is "all in all" (1 Cor 15:28). In the words of St. Irenaeus, writing in his *Against Heresies* (4.20.7), "If the glory of God is the fully living human being, the fullness of that life is the vision of God" (*Gloria dei vivens homo; vita autem hominis est visio dei*). As the psalmist sings, the redeemed will

> feast on the abundance of your house,
> and you give them drink from the river of your delights.
> For with you is the fountain of life;
> in your light we see light. (Ps 36:8)

In his confrontation with the bounded world of the Sadducees, Jesus strikingly expresses his sense of God as the source of endless life. The life-giving power of God is in no way limited by death (see Mark 12:18-27; Matt 22:23-33; Luke 20:27-38). As Jesus argues,

> And the fact that the dead are raised Moses himself showed, in the story about the bush, when he speaks of the Lord as the God of Abraham, the God of Isaac, and the God of Jacob. *Now he is God not of the dead, but of the living; for to him all of them are alive.*" (Luke 20:37-38; emphasis added)

The issue here is the character of God and the nature of eternal life. Whatever the inevitable process of decay in this biological form of life, for God the human person is endlessly alive. The fact that the great patriarchs of Israel, as well as our ancestors, are dead for us does not mean they are dead in the sight of God. Nor, for that matter, do they need to be dead for the Christian community in any ultimate sense. God is Life: to be with God is to live. For those living in a death-bound world, living means not being dead. For those given over to God, living means union with God, the source and goal of life, in this life, in death, and after death. The deathless vitality of God is the all-determining consideration. From a New Testament perspective, whether we live or whether we die, we are always alive to God and we belong to Christ (1 Cor 3:22; Phil 1:20). In a radical sense, heaven, as eternal life, has already begun. Our real lives are "hidden with Christ in God" (Col 3:3). To God, the infinite ocean of life and love, no one is ever just "dead," least of all when they die. Clearly, Jesus radiated a sense of the boundless ebullience of divine life and of the unending life that would result from surrendering to the source and goal of all the living. Heaven, from this point of view, is our full awakening to that life, in the company of all those who have lived for God.

Theology always needs to be both humble and creative, especially when dealing with what is beyond the scope of any human eye, ear, or imagination (see 1 Cor 2:9). When this reverent, negative kind of affirmation is forgotten, the life of heaven is trivialized. But the reality of what is to come is also suggested positively through the interplay of many rich images. These are drawn from nature, as with the garden of Paradise, the stream of living water, the light of God, and so forth. Interweaving with such natural images are those of a more cultural kind, such as the heavenly city, the throne of God, the new covenant, the temple and sacrifice. These, in turn, interact with images of personal union when the Scriptures refer to mutual indwelling and use terms associated with marriage, family, communion in the Spirit, and the Body of Christ. A dominant analogy is the great banquet. Then, there is the image that has most deeply affected the Christian sense of heavenly fulfillment, and it is drawn from our experience of enlightenment and vision: we will see God "face to face." In this exuberant interplay of images and symbols, each evokes some aspect of eternal life.

The culminating display of God's love cannot be reduced to any one of these images. Given the limited human capacity to envisage "what God has prepared for those who love him" (1 Cor 2:9), we must keep all these scriptural images in play. We must allow them to point beyond themselves to what can never be expressed. A sense of heaven as life with God is distorted when we pretend to know too much. Nonetheless, the tradition of faith and hope points us in the right direction.

For instance, heaven is the moment in which God's self-giving purpose is fulfilled. Our limited imaginations are inclined to think of God as the infinite object that we finally reach by living well. But what is easily overlooked is that our going to heaven is first of all God's coming to us. God is the first and final Giver. The Holy Trinity is lovingly involved in every moment of the life of each and all, to draw each human being into the divine life. When John declares that "God is love" (1 John 4:8, 16), he goes on to remind us that it is not as though we first loved God, but that God has first loved us (1 John 4:10). In other words, the divine initiative is always the determining factor in bringing our lives to their destined fulfillment. The God-given gifts of faith, hope, and love are looking to the final gift of God. The Love that God is embraces the beginning and the end of human existence as it unfolds in freedom and grows in loving. In the human mind and heart the mystery of God comes into its own. God will be "all in all" as the Trinity draws creation into its own life.

Jesus does not cease to be the mediator between God and us in this final outpouring of Love. He does not drop into the background now the goal is reached. He remains "the way" (John 14:6). For in the end there will be the shining forth of what has been true all along: "No one comes to the Father except through me" (John 14:6). In the vision of God, the blessed see God precisely as the Father of our Lord Jesus Christ, and they share in the joy of his relationship with the Father: "If you know me, you will know my Father also" (John 14:7). Those who have followed Christ as "the way" will find him revealed as "the truth and the life" (John 14:6). God is seen as the self-giving Love that was incarnate in Christ in order to gather all into one (John 17:22-23). Our face-to-face vision of God is to see God in the face of Christ: "For it is the God who said, 'Let light shine out of darkness,' who has shone in our hearts to give the light of the knowledge of the glory of God in the face of Jesus Christ" (2 Cor 4:6). Far from making Christ disappear into the shadows, the radiance of the divine light never loses its luminous focus in Christ.

In this perspective, heaven is the space fashioned for us by Christ within the divine life. It is no extraterrestrial location, but the final dimension of creation. It includes the spiritual and material dimensions of the universe. By making all this his own, Christ has introduced every dimension of existence into the divine realm. The Word has himself taken on our humanity and made it his own. In Christ's rising from the dead, he has not left our humanity or our world behind. In him the whole universe has become a new creation. As Paul wrote of Christ: "He is the image of the invisible God, the firstborn of all creation; for in him all things in heaven and on earth . . . have been created through him and for him. He himself is before all things, and in him all things hold together" (Col 1:15-17).

In the full unfolding of the paschal mystery of his life, death, and resurrection, Christ will be revealed as the ultimate factor in the destiny and form of creation. All created energies and forces are made subject to him, reintegrated into a new wholeness (e.g., Eph 1:10; Col 1:15-20; John 1:1-5). In and through him, the reshaping of the universe has irreversibly begun. Christ himself is the supremely personal space in which all the becoming of history and world takes place. In this regard, he is the absolute point by which all else is measured, the goal finalizing all genetic processes. Faith in the risen One affects our sense of the final shape of reality—the world is already on the way to transformation.

Heaven is the world transformed by Love. The mission of the Spirit of Love is to inspire love. This Love subsumes, transforms and fulfills all the loves that make up our lives. The quality of any life is most revealed in its loves: "Where your treasure is, there your heart will be also" (Matt 6:21). What is spontaneously called "real life" is essentially found in the loves and relationships that make up that life in its interpersonal, social, or global dimensions. Admittedly, the experience of love has its own ambiguities. The erotomania of contemporary Western culture immediately reduces all love to sexual relationships. Given, too, the present fragility of marriage and family life, the experience of love is frequently associated with pain and the possibilities of self-destruction. Love, even if it is the most precious intimation of eternal life, has been often compromised by darker forebodings.

Still, there is something overwhelmingly positive. For anyone in love, not only the beloved other but other persons—even formerly ordinary words, places, and gestures, as well as the body itself—are transformed. Everything is suffused with a new energy and enchantment. Isolated individuality is dissolved; one's whole being expands. There is a loss of self, of the independent and isolated self—but only for the sake of finding this self transformed in a transfigured world. The Canticle of Canticles, literally, "the Greatest Song of All," remains the classical biblical affirmation of this fundamental ecstatic feature of human existence: "I am my beloved's, and his desire is for me" (Cant 7:10). To the lover, the world is a new creation, even if hitherto unknown and unrecognized. To be in love is to experience intimations of eternity and of finally coming home. It is the most evocative, and perhaps the most neglected, anticipation of the life of heaven. For all the loves of our heart are homing to a final fulfillment. Heaven is when our Godward hearts come home and find their peace. Eternal life is the ultimate state of being-in-love. In this it shares in the Love-life that God is.

The eternal life of heaven is love—and light. There is the face-to-face vision of God. St. Paul writes, "For now we see in a mirror, dimly, but then we will see face to face. Now I know only in part; then I will know fully, even as I have been fully known" (1 Cor 13:12). In the light of glory, the Love that God is enables the finite human mind to receive the radiance of the divine mystery into itself.

The blessed are transformed in God. They participate in the light of God's own self-knowledge. This overflowing radiance contrasts with our present mode of existence. Even in the holiest life there remains a basic limitation in the human capacity to see God. Even if we are lovingly united to the will of God, the face of God is unseen. It is shrouded in what the mystics refer to as the "the cloud of unknowing."

But all limitations are overcome when the blessed "see" God in an immediate, face-to-face knowledge. In a final act of grace, the divine Word is given into the human mind so as to expand its capacities to receive the light of God. In that way, the human mind catches up with the reality of its love. In a final vision, the mystery that love had lived is disclosed in its full clarity. What was loved in darkness is now known in light; and love is transformed into the joy and peace of possession. Those who now see God possess in the deepest sense an inside knowledge of God.

The life of heaven is not like being on the outside, as though looking onto or into the reality of God. It means having an inside knowledge, being ecstatically immersed in the ocean of Light. And so, to be "in heaven" is to feast on the reality of God and to drink from the source of life. It is to taste the sweetness of the Spirit and to inhale its fragrance. It is to be plunged into the depths of divine mystery. It is to hear the eternal music of the Word and touch and embrace what in life could never be grasped and to be bathed in the beauty of the Light. In that vision the blessed not only see God face to face but also see the whole created universe, in every dimension of its being and becoming, as the continuing and creative self-manifestation of the Love from which it came and in which it finds its goal. Caught up into such infinities, the human spirit finds its basic delight in knowing that God—Father, Son, and Holy Spirit—is truly God, mystery unbounded.

VII

The full-bodied reality of God's love for us necessarily looks to the resurrection of the body. God's love is not for souls only.

The eternal life to which love looks is a heaven as the home of the totally human. The risen Lord himself appeared not as a ghost but as the newly embodied source and form of an existence totally transformed in the Spirit. To share in his resurrection is to find that the joy of love and the light of vision overflow to transfigure our bodily being. As was previously remarked, human beings are never purely spiritual beings. Without some form of embodiment, the human person can scarcely be said to exist. As bodily beings, our existence is immersed in the totality of the world. Hence, hope justifiably envisages the resurrection of the body as conformed to the body of the risen Lord: "He will transform the body of our humiliation that it may be conformed to the body of his glory, by the power that also enables him to make all things subject to himself" (Phil 3:21). United with the Lord in his death, faith yields to the Spirit of a new creation:

> If the Spirit of him who raised Jesus from the dead dwells in you, he who raised Christ from the dead will give life to your mortal bodies also through his Spirit that dwells in you. (Rom 8:11)

Hope in God's love can hardly claim to be "catholic" if it leaves out our bodily rootedness in this material cosmos. Part of the problem is the limitations in our way of imagining what our bodies are. We are inclined to think of the human body as a particular personal possession, a self-contained unit separate from the rest of the world. In contrast to that extreme material individualism is a more relational perspective. Through the body the human person is inserted into a universe, a cosmic totality. The body represents, then, not so much a boundary but the focal point of a network of relationships extending to the whole physical universe. The embodied human person is earthed and grounded in the whole, and the whole is enriched by what each one is. The resurrection of the body is, therefore, of cosmic significance.

In other words, to be in the heaven of God's revealed love is to be "somebody" in a transformed universe. We are destined not to be disembodied spirits haunting the world to come but to be fully human within it. Even so, we do not cling to this present state of biological existence. Still, it promises more than meets the eye. An analogical understanding of what is to come must have some continuity with our present experience of the body in this temporal form of life. It is a biophysical, ever-changing metabolic unit serving this particular stage of our human existence. Through the body we enjoy a relational and self-expressive participation in the world and its history. Yet there are discontinuities as well. Paul has already reminded us of this: "What is sown is perishable, what is raised is imperishable. . . . It is sown a physical body, it is raised a spiritual body" (1 Cor 15:42, 44; cf. 15:35-58).

Resurrection does not mean resuscitation; it means transformation in a creation transformed in the Spirit in the pattern of Christ's resurrection. A new form of embodiment is involved. The seed of eternal life is germinating in our present earthly existence and already begins to breathe in the free air of a world made new by God's love.

Already there are tokens of the transformation in store for all creation. In the minds of our great thinkers, this world becomes a universe present to itself as boundless wonder. To inspired artists, it offers shapes and colors, sounds and movements to burst forth into ever new forms. In our mystics, it is world come home to itself as something holy, a vast sacrament bearing within itself the presence of all-creative mystery. In human science and craft, it yields itself to human use as no longer a blind force threatening humankind but as the earth nurturing the emergence of a planetary humanity. The mystery of the cosmos has smiled on us in the wonder of a human face and has given birth to each of us from the womb of a woman. It has given man and woman to each other in the life-giving intimacy and shared joy of sexual love. This material universe has become, as it were, the shared body of the human spirit. To hope for the resurrection of the body implies, then, a cosmic hope of being saved with, and in, our world.

Because the human spirit is embodied in a material world, that world of matter is being lifted to new levels of being through the activity of the human mind and heart and hand. Indeed, in the incarnation of the Word, the material world has been occupied and possessed from within by the divine mystery itself. In the resurrection of Christ, it has become the beginning of a new creation. Neither for the New Adam nor for us who believe in him can heaven mean leaving this world behind. All the groaning of the cosmos will yield to the "Alleluia!" of a creation finally at home with its Creator. St. Ambrose of Milan, writing on the death of his brother Satyrus, sums up the cosmic sweep of the mystery of Christ: "In Christ's resurrection the world arose. In Christ's resurrection, the heavens arose, in Christ's resurrection the earth itself arose."[2]

VIII

Here the Catholic doctrine of Mary assumed body and soul into heaven has special significance. For the assumption of Mary is a concrete symbol of the creativity of our Love-charged world. Early patristic theology thought of Mary as the New Eve formed from the New Adam (cf. Gen 2:21-13), as the "mother of all the living" (Gen 3:20). Against such a background, the assumption is a unique Marian privilege. On the other hand, being now assumed into the glory of Christ, she is the anticipation of the heaven of a transfigured creation. She is the paradigm instance of creation surrendered to the all-creative mystery of God. As the Mother of Christ, she symbolizes the generativity of creation as it is penetrated by the Spirit. In her, the Advent prayer, as it echoes the words of the great prophet Isaiah, has been answered: "[L]et the earth be opened and bring forth a savior."[3] Her assumption nourishes hope with an assurance that our nature and our history have already come to term in Christ. She embodies the reality of our world as having received into itself the mystery that is to transform the universe in its entirety. Through her assumption into glory, our world has already become heaven.

It is not as though a wondrous transformation of the material world is totally beyond our experience. Every time we sing, speak, dance, make music, or paint, the sounds and colors and movements of the natural world breathe with new life. The arts bring about a higher, more human embodiment in the world of cultural communication. The notes on a page plot the emergence of a symphony, as instruments made of metal, wood, and animal tissue work together with human skill and imagination to produce a great musical event. The energies of matter have been tapped to provide human intelligence with possibilities of communication, as with the World Wide Web. The creative human spirit is ever infusing matter with life and meaning and bringing about a new level of embodiment. When we speak of the resurrection of the body, the relevant question—even if it can never be fully answered, given the limits of our present experience—is this: How might the divine Creator Spirit penetrate and refashion the world of matter so as to bring into being a risen body appropriate to life in Christ? Answering that question would mean thinking of the material constitution of body in another dimension outside the space-time continuum of our present existence. Moreover, in the current science of matter, mass and energy are interrelated. Subatomic entities exhibit both particle-like and wave-like features. In the world of relativity, the "laws" of time and space as we experience them in the familiar sensory world are strangely indeterminate when it comes to the innermost constitution of matter as quantum physics would describe it. The imaginative language of current physics already begins to sound like a description of the glorified body as the medievals spoke of it in terms of "subtlety," "agility," "radiance," and so forth. But the point remains: Love is reshaping the universe in its entirety. It looks to the full-bodied fullness of eternal life in God. Then, the scattered notes of our lives will be brought together in one great symphony of praise and thanksgiving to the glory of God. God's love keeps forever all that is good. In the words of the Second Vatican Council's Pastoral Constitution on the Church in the Modern World (*Gaudium et Spes*),

> When we have spread on earth the fruits of our nature and our enterprise—human dignity, sisterly and brotherly communion, and freedom—according to the command of the Lord and in his Spirit, we will find them once again, cleansed this time from stain of sin, illuminated and transfigured, when Christ presents to his Father an eternal and universal kingdom 'of truth and life, a kingdom of holiness and grace, a kingdom of justice, love and peace.' Here on earth the kingdom is mysteriously present; when the Lord comes it will enter into its perfection. (GS 39)

The self-giving love of God looks to a final consummation. All our capacities to follow the summons of true life, to be more than the limited versions of our social and cultural identities, come to fulfillment and rest in the full display of God's love: "For with you is the fountain of life; in your light we see light" (Ps 36:9).

Conclusion

 The foregoing brief chapters make up a meditation on what it means to identify God as Love. That meaning radiates out through the seven irreplaceable terms we have considered, just as each of them converges in the affirmation that God is Love. Each of these names/terms is a necessary telling point in the story of how God so loves the world:

- the Father as the source of all love
- the Son as the personal self-gift of the Father to the world
- the cross as the unconditional character of God's love
- the resurrection as Love's victory and transformative power
- the Holy Spirit as the continuing outpouring of love for every generation
- the church as the gathering of those who believe in the love revealed and surrender to it
- the eternal life that this love promises

The result is that we have a brief formula centered in the Love that God is that can be unfolded in the terms just described. How further elaboration might take place will depend on the context of a particular Christian communication, be it in a community, in the larger ecumenical situation, or in the emerging challenges related to interfaith meetings.

The order in which these ideas have been presented in this exposition follows pretty much the usual sequence found in biblical and creedal accounts of God's saving grace for the world. On the other hand, it is worth stressing once more that in the interests of a theology working in a particular situation, we could start with any of these seven terms—as long as all were eventually included. As we mentioned in the introduction, leaving out any one of them results in a gross distortion of the Christian story. Likewise, concentrating on any one of them to the exclusion of the rest leads to a similar sorry outcome.

However, there is plenty of flexibility. Some might wish, for instance, to give a greater emphasis on the Holy Spirit. That could mean starting with the experience of the Holy Spirit in the corporate consciousness of the *church*. It would look back to the role of the Spirit in Christ's life, *death*, and *resurrection*. It would show how the Holy Spirit inspires a free and intimate relationship to the *Father*, forming believers into the image of the *Son*. Underlying all this would be an appreciation of the gift of the Spirit as a fountain of living water springing up to *eternal life* (John 4:14)—and so all terms would be included.

Needless to say, these reflections on God as Love cannot replace the patient scholarship of theology with its many specializations. What it does offer, however, is a way of sturdily re-centering the theological and spiritual focus of our concerns so that Christian faith emerges as ever new—and so to be newly owned and freshly explored. The seven headings we have used serve as signposts of exploration into "the breadth and length and height and depth" (Eph 3:18) of God's love, the first and last thing in every moment of Christian existence.

A deep appreciation of the truth of the statement "God is Love" presupposes a continuing effort to rethink everything we receive from our biblical, Christian, religious, and philosophical resources. There is no need to replace the wisdom of the ages that spoke in a larger and more varied vocabulary: God is sheer Be-ing, supreme goodness, infinite beauty, all-wise, "omnipotent," and so forth—many of the terms we have already used. Our specifically Christian focus on God as Love arises from faith in Christ as the self-revelation of God and his self-giving love. There is a particularity and concreteness implied when the Scriptures assert that "the Word became flesh and lived among us" (John 1:14), "in him the whole fullness of the deity dwells bodily" (Col 2:9), or "in Christ God was reconciling the world to himself" (2 Cor 5:19). Such particular statements refer to an individual human existence, that of Jesus of Nazareth, and to the geographical and historical location of his life and death—and the manner of his death, execution under Pontius Pilate.

The recognition of the particularity in time and space of God's self-revelation in Christ originally provoked the amazement expressed in the phrase "God is Love." Yet it is an amazement born out of awe. The infinite God, the God of limitless goodness and beauty, of power and intelligence, the creator of all that is, the One in whom "we live and move and have our being" (Acts 17:28), has shown himself in such a way as to be named as "Love." The wonder of God's love can never be exhausted. True, a certain kind of emotionally repressive fixation can occur when all the emphasis falls on the idea of love in a monodimensional way. It is suspiciously close to a self-regarding human projection, basically unaware of God's sheer initiative. In other words, this most radical biblical sentence can be reduced to meaning "love is God." A superficial sentimentality can take over—romantic at best, self-serving at worst. When the awe-inspiring transcendence of God is swallowed up into mere sentiment, a growing caution marks the interpretation of this biblical phrase.

But that is less likely to happen when the full vocabulary of God's love is kept in mind so as to include the seven considerations followed in this exposition. Still, it is important to use this phrase in a manner that appreciates its profound theological significance. That means allowing the emphasis to return to the subject of the sentence: "*God* is Love." How might this proper emphasis be achieved?

Reflecting on the infinite being, goodness, wisdom, and omnipotence of God would certainly throw light on how God relates to us and the world in the most intimate, generous way of love. The ground would be cleared of sentimental and self-serving projections. More importantly, it would become clear that God is not one more "thing" within the fabric of the world. The great negatives must come into play: God is not finite; nor is God limited, impotent, or unknowing in regard to our world and the happenings that make it up. This is not the time, however, at the conclusion of this little book, to embark on a full treatment of, say, the divine attributes. But some things can be said.

Take the notion of God's love itself. We have touched on this point in chapter 2, speaking of the special character of the Father's love. Everything comes into being out of the sheer abundance of God's generative and creative love. We noted the profound truth in saying that God created the universe "out of nothing." When God creates, there is nothing first "there" for God to work on. In other words, God creates "out of love," out of pure love. All that is has been loved into being and is to be received as a sheer gift from the heart of God. All the created universe is the manifestation of sheer loving on the part of God. St. Thomas makes an illuminating contrast between human love and God's love:

> Because our will is not the cause of the goodness in things, but is attracted by the goodness of some object, our love . . . is not the cause of goodness itself, but rather goodness, whether it is truly or only apparently so, provokes our love. . . . In contrast, God's love pours forth and creates the goodness in everything. (*Summa Theologica* I, q. 20, a. 2)

To understand this is to recognize everything and everyone as a gift emanating from the creative Love that God is. We are what we are because of the self-giving love welling up from the heart of God. No human merits are presupposed—no "raw material," not even good behavior on our part. All is grace.

"God is Love" is the meaningful point of convergence for the names and events essential to specifically Christian faith. This basic affirmation serves also to focus the great classic tradition of theology speaking of God in terms of the divine "attributes"—as when we say God is all-powerful, all-wise, and infinitely good and beautiful. Each of such attributes sharpens and extends that perception of faith in God as Love. For example, God exercises infinite power as the Love that keeps on being Love out of the infinite resources of the divine goodness and wisdom. The truth and reality of this God find their most personal and intimate expression when, in the consciousness of God-given faith, we confess that God is Love. The all-surpassing knowledge and freedom of God are implied in the very terms of revelation. But the most concrete expression of who God is and how God acts is found in the manner in which God confronts the power of evil. An inexhaustible love and mercy are revealed. The saving will of God immeasurably surpasses the power of evil. It releases the burden of sin and guilt and breathes hope into the hopelessness of human failure and defeat.

The horizon of Love keeps everything within the radiance of divine beauty. This does not mean that we are presented merely with a lovely idea or a beautiful expression. God's self-revelation is a communication of infinite mystery. It comes to us with the imposing and attractive power of a great work of art. The Gospel is something like a great poem or symphony of love, forgiveness, and healing. It comes to us in the face of Christ, in the beauty of creation itself, and in the drama of all the lives, saints and sinners, who are each part of the history of faith.

St. Thomas would say that the most suitable name for God is "the One who is." By "is" he means that God is sheer "To Be" (*esse* in Latin is a verb). We can communicate a sense of what this means by saying that God is pure "is-ness," unlimited "Be-ing," the infinite "Act" involved in all that is and will be. As sheer Be-ing, God is the fount and support of all that is. Each being exists in a certain way—as, say, an atom, a flower, a bird, a human being, or an angel. But God is Be-ing without limit, outside all such determinations. In the words of scholastic philosophy, the infinite Be-ing of God is outside every "genus." The infinite cannot be specified by the finite.

This notion of God as limitless, unbounded, ever-actual Be-ing means that God, the source of being, is present as the giver of being at the heart of all beings. Nothing that exists has the power to initiate its own existence and to sustain itself in being. In everyone, in everything everywhere, infinite Be-ing is present as the source and sustainer of all that is.

The depth of this sense of God as limitless Be-ing clears the ground, as it were, for a deeper appreciation of God as Love. The infinite fullness of divine Be-ing, in the joy of perfect peace and self-possession, has freely chosen to be "our God," the God of *this* creation, chosen out of limitless possibilities. The infinite Mystery has freely chosen to disclose its otherwise invisible face in Christ. An unconditional, self-giving Love now draws us into sharing in the divine life.

The infinities of God's grace in Christ are never exhausted. It is time for a more creative catholicity on the part of the church in its mission to all nations. How that will work out for future generations is not given to us to know—even though the abiding reality is "Jesus Christ . . . the same yesterday and today and forever" (Heb 13:8). The God of love is never about to abandon his people. The Father's self-giving in the Son and the Spirit is irreversible. His love is not exhausted with past generations or with this one or with those of the future. The Spirit is ever at work, declaring "the things that are to come" (John 16:13).

If future ages look back, they will see how much of our present efforts have inevitably fallen short. Perhaps they will detect in our actions and attitudes grave distortions and misplaced efforts to hurry or limit the ways of God. Still, the church of the future will be sympathetic to our pilgrim condition and will understand what it cost to face the complex issues of our time. What we can bequeath to the future, therefore, will be all the more valuable if we can cut through the complexity to the deepest truth and hand it on as a little more deeply understood, treasured, and lived: God is Love.

Even this simple working theology must be mainly concerned with the future. Of course, the ultimate future is in the hands of God—the final event of revelation, of God "all in all." In the meantime, there is the future in the obvious temporal sense—and that is what, as we pray and think and work, we must keep steadily in mind in order to serve the needs of coming generations. They will need more than a record of the problems and conflicts of this time.

Dividing fellow Christians along conservative or progressive lines has outlived its usefulness. The critical division now is between those who commit themselves to live deeply from center and those who are superficial, who float free, unanchored in any depth. We have all been pretty much occupied with the new questions arising out of today's secular, scientific, and pluralistic environment. We have felt the grief of the collapse of any coherent European-style Christendom. We have tried to put the best construction on the changes that have occurred and to diagnose the enormity of our problems.

In the face of all this, there have been courageous attempts to promote a many-sided development of the great tradition of faith. Every generation is confronted with a cruel choice as to what deserves its attention, given the shortness of time and the limits of human capacities. The resources of the past have never been more available, but the demands of the present are ever more urgent.

The problem is one of responding to these urgent demands even while most of us can claim only a very thin and distant familiarity with the past in all its richness. The simplest and truest stance for faith is not to be conservative in an anxious sense but to go to the deepest point and to live unconditionally from there. To be giddily confronted with what is called "the postmodern world" is to find that nothing stays in place and that everything has to be newly discovered in a world of fragments, unfinished meaning, and forgotten voices. *That* is not necessarily a bad position for Christian witness—as long as it doesn't undermine the most elemental convictions of Christian faith and distract from its most radical spiritual experience.

In the end, Love has breathed life and love into us. It calls forth a complete and unreserved "Amen." It will be the Amen of each of us living and dying into the ever-expanding community of the faithful from generation to generation. It is the Amen of response to the gift that has been given and to the Love that has revealed itself in Christ. From beginning to end, he is "the Alpha and the Omega" (Rev 22:13), the first and last letter of the alphabet of Christian existence. In him we find the "Yes" to all God's promises and the "Amen" to all our praying and believing (2 Cor 1:20; cf. Rev 3:14). As the power working in every aspect of our existence, "it is God who establishes us with you in Christ and has anointed us, by putting his seal on us and giving his Spirit in our hearts as a first instalment" (2 Cor 1:21-22).

Love unfolds in its many dimensions. Amen to each of them:

> To the Source of all love in the Father, Amen!
> To the self-gift of love in the Son, Amen!
> To the boundless mercy of love in the cross, Amen!
> To the victory of love in the resurrection, Amen!
> To the Spirit of love breathing through all time and space, Amen!
> To the celebration of such love in the church, Amen!
> To the glory of love in the life of the world to come, Amen!

Notes

PREFACE (pages vii–ix)
   1. Benedict XVI, *Deus Caritas Est* (December 25, 2005), no. 1.

CHAPTER 2 (pages 10–25)
   1. See, for example, John 1:18; 3:16, 35; 4:23, 34; 5:18-21, 26-28, 30, 36-37; 6:32-33, 37-40, 44-45, 57, 65; 7:16.
   2. Ibid.
   3. John Chrysostom, *In S. Martyrem Ignatium*, bk. 1, PG 50:588.
   4. Ignatius of Antioch, "A Letter to the Romans," in Cyril C. Richardson, ed., *Early Christian Writings* (New York: Macmillan, 1970), 105.

CHAPTER 3 (pages 26–37)
   1. J. Neuner, SJ, and J. Dupuis, SJ, eds., *The Christian Faith in the Doctrinal Documents of the Catholic Church*, rev. ed. (New York: Alba House, 1982), 154, n. 614.
   2. Ibid., 154, n. 615.

CHAPTER 4 (pages 38–49)
   1. Influenced by the anthropology of René Girard, both James Alison, *Raising Abel: The Recovery of the Eschatological Imagination* (New York: Crossroad, 1996), and, more generally, Gil Bailie, *Violence Unveiled: Humanity at the Crossroads* (New York: Crossroad, 1997), make this point.
   2. For this translation, see F. J. Moloney, *Glory Not Dishonor: Reading John 13–21* (Minneapolis: Fortress Press, 1998), 13, n. 39.

CHAPTER 5 (pages 50–63)

   1. This is the Aramaic. The NRSV translates this as "Our Lord, come!"

CHAPTER 8 (pages 95–109)

   1. *Catechism of the Catholic Church* (Vatican City: Libreria Editrice Vaticana, 1994), no. 1020.

   2. Ambrose of Milan, *De excessu fratris sui*, bk. 1, PL 16:1354.

   3. Entrance antiphon for the Fourth Sunday of Advent. Cf. Isa. 45:8.

Index